# HELLO AUTISM

## How To Love Like and Learn From Your Special Needs Child

Theresa M. Noye

Hello Autism: How To Love Like And Learn From Your Special Needs Child
www.theresanoye.com



ISBN: 979-8-63786-427-0



Limits of Liability and Disclaimer of Warranty
The author and publisher shall not be liable for your misuse of the enclosed material. This book is strictly for informational and educational purposes only.

Warning – Disclaimer
The purpose of this book is to educate and entertain. The author and/or publisher do not guarantee that anyone following these techniques, suggestions, tips, ideas, or strategies will become successful. The author and/or publisher shall have neither liability nor responsibility to anyone with respect to any loss or damage caused, or alleged to be caused, directly or indirectly by the information contained in this book.

Medical Disclaimer
The medical or health information in this book is provided as an information resource only, and is not to be used or relied on for any diagnostic or treatment purposes. This information is not intended to be patient education, does not create any patient-physician relationship, and should not be used as a substitute for professional diagnosis and treatment.

Publisher
10-10-10 Publishing
Markham, ON   Canada

Printed in Canada and the United States of America

# Table of Contents

*Dedicated to the parents and caretakers of special needs children. You are a force of nature. You possess the seeds of resiliency, inspiration, innovation, persistence, kindness, and love. You make the world a better place...one day at a time.*

*&*

*To my father, the late Elder Carl Michael Blades. I am you.*
*I feel your strength, focus, and creativity with me every day.*
*I hear your voice calling me to fulfill my purpose.*
*Thank you. I love you Poppy.*

# Foreword

Are you, or someone you know and love, dealing with the realities of parenting today? More specifically, are you the parent of a child with special needs? Do you desire to grow, heal and be inspired as a result of your life experience but you feel so frozen by fear that you aren't sure which way to turn?

Would you like to discover your own, and your child's, mission on this planet and do it while you become happier, emotionally healthier, and tap into the regenerating power of hope? Would you like to learn more about the boundless power you possess to envision and shape a vibrant and cathartic life for you and your child?

If you are considering parenting under these daunting circumstances, you need to know how to overcome the variety of internal and external obstacles that threaten to drain your joy, peace and contentment.

No matter who you are or what your current situation as the loved one or caregiver for a special needs child, regardless of your age, culture, beliefs or religion, *Hello Autism: How to Love, Like and Learn From Your Special Needs Child* is full of insights, and will act as a guide in your life, advising you on the steps to take before you navigate your challenges, and teaching you how to fulfill your incredible purpose.

Author Theresa Noye began her journey over fifteen years ago when her son was diagnosed with Autism. She understands intellectually and experientially the doubt, guilt, fear, shame and embarrassment you face on a daily basis. After making the decision to embrace her challenge she was able to change the way she thought, which produced radical changes for her, and her entire family. She is a great example of what you can accomplish as a parent of a special needs child when you apply everything she teaches you within this book.

From her own experiences as a parent, as well as the experience she has gained in her nearly two decades of assisting others to grow from adversity, Theresa has written *Hello Autism: How to Love, Like and Learn From Your Special Needs Child,* so that you can turn your struggle into success, just as she did.

Theresa shares her personal experiences with you to help you to overcome fear and move to the place you wish to be. She believes that having a child with a special needs diagnosis is not in your hands, but what you do thereafter is your decision and responsibility. This book will help you to settle the torrents in your mind and focus on creating your best outcome for both you and your child.

Get ready to read this amazing journey and create a massive change in your life and your child's life, and inspire everyone you know.

**Raymond Aaron**
**New York Times Bestselling Author**

# Introduction

If you are reading this book, chances are you have a child with autism, or know someone with autism. I didn't know anything about autism before I had Regal. I never even thought about the special needs community until I had a child with special needs. I like to consider myself a *good* person, but before having Regal, I laughed at inappropriate jokes, subconsciously avoided people that were different, and gave the evil eye to parents with loud, disruptive, and seemingly rude children.

As humans, our experiences are catalysts for powerful change. The Civil Rights Movement, March for Our Lives, Domestic Violence Awareness Month, and Race for the Cure are just a few examples of movements making an impact, born out of a personal experience. When there is an emotional connection to an issue, it moves us to respond to a need. Our greatest struggles and painful moments become opportunities for awareness, transformation, and connection. Autism has done that for me and my family.

I am the woman I am today because I have had the privilege of parenting a son on the autism spectrum. I discovered my purpose, connected with the goodness of people, and experienced firsthand the transformative power of love. Parenting my special son has moved me from approaching each day with the question, "Why autism?" to living with hopeful expectation, and exclaiming, "Hello autism!"

And that's why I had to write this book. Having a child with special needs is challenging, and that's an understatement. However, it is not a life sentence. Yes, this book will give you strategies for choosing to enjoy life when it does not go according to plan. I have given you tools and exercises to guide you throughout the book. But more importantly, it will give you a different perspective. It challenges you to embrace the lessons that your child and those around are waiting to teach you. What would it be like to greet each day with "Hello, autism! What will you teach me today?"

Every one of us is unique. Every child on the spectrum is different. This is not a cookie-cutter, one-size-fits-all. However, as human beings, there is always a common thread. We are more alike than we are different. So I ask you read with an open heart. If what you are currently doing is not working for you, it's time to try something new. These are my experiences. Take what resonates with you, and leave behind what doesn't. At the end of each chapter is a place for you to jot down your thoughts, ideas, and insights. Don't attempt to do everything at once. Test it out over time.

This is a love journey for you and your child. Although everyone's path is different, love will always lead you. You can never lose love; and that, my friend, is true for everyone.

# Chapter One

# What's Wrong With My Son?

*"My mother is not a CIA agent, but she's an Italian mother, and she'd do anything for her son."*
– Adriano Giannini

## Born Perfect

I never wanted kids. When I was little, I would strip my dolls, line them up, and beat them. In graduate school, I had a job in a day care center, and I got sick every day. I hated being there. I probably shouldn't have been working there, but it paid well. I would appreciate the cuteness of kids, but I did not enjoy them. And babies...they were even worse. I don't even think I held a baby before I had my own... well, besides my little sister. Babies weren't my thing.

Then I fell in love with my husband, Henry, and we got married. Love changed me. It made me want to give myself in ways I had previously resisted. I allowed myself to be vulnerable. I felt safe. I felt accepted. I knew I could be myself and Henry would still love me. We spent our first five years of marriage loving each other, learning about each other, and enjoying each other. That kind of love makes you do crazy things...like having a baby. As we grew in our love for each other, I wanted to give myself to this way of loving. Having a child was a byproduct of our love. I miscarried our first pregnancy. It was rough, but we loved each other through it. My second pregnancy was successful. Barring an emergency C-section, all went well, and I had a beautiful boy. We named him Regal Aaron Noye. He was perfect. He had a full head of hair and his eyes were piercing. I looked at him and only wanted to love and protect him. There was a sacredness around his birth. It was amazing that I was a part of the miracle of life. This being came from the love of me and Henry. He was entrusted to us. I was honored and grateful.

I left the hospital, and we were proud parents. My mother stayed with us for a month. Since I had a C-section, I needed time to recover. I also needed to learn how to care for a newborn. I was clueless. Like I said, I never cared for babies. Mom showed me the ropes. But what I discovered was that I already had what I needed. She showed me some practical things, like how to change a diaper, how to hold the baby, and how to get organized and put a system in place. She taught me to establish a routine, making sure to leave the house and do something each day. But just being with her and spending time together as a new mom was priceless. I gained a newfound appreciation for her, as my mother and as a woman.

I also learned that God had placed inside of me an innate ability to connect with Regal. I had natural abilities. I had intuition. I could hear his cries and sense what he wanted. I was able to hold him and rock him in just the right way. My voice intuitively adapted to the right tone and pitch to soothe him. Words came out of me that he responded to. Regal was pretty laid back. He smiled and laughed easily. He was reaching his developmental goals, according to the pediatrician. And he walked before he crawled, which to me and Henry, made him a genius. But there were other things that we began to notice—actually that my husband noticed. He wasn't talking. He was making sounds, but he wasn't talking to us. My husband was really concerned, but I figured he was developing at his own pace. After all, he was our first child. He didn't have an older sibling to model. As far as I was concerned, my son was perfect. But was he?

## Ignoring the Signs

Henry was adamant about discussing Regal's progress with our family physician. I reluctantly took him in for a visit. The doctor agreed with me and told us we shouldn't be concerned. Every child develops at their own pace. I gave myself an invisible pat on the back and focused on not having a "see I was right" look on my face. Henry, however, would not accept this and insisted that Regal be evaluated further. The doctor gave us information for the Early Intervention Unit. I convinced Henry to wait a little bit. I wanted to put Regal in preschool and get him around other kids. I was sure that he just needed the right environment. I was completely ignoring the signs. Regal was 2 years old. He was around other kids in church, and when we were at events with our friends and colleagues, there were opportunities for him to engage with other kids, but he didn't. There was something going on, but I didn't want to see it.

I enrolled him in a preschool, and there was an orientation where the kids had to come and play with each other. The parents were encouraged to sit and watch. It was in that moment that I realized that Regal was different. He was not playing with the kids. He was in his own world, laughing and talking to himself in his own language. I felt like everyone was looking at me. I imagined that all the parents were wondering what was wrong with my son. I was convinced that they were all thinking that we did not belong there. I wanted to get up and show him how to play. I wanted to make him interact with the kids. For the first time, I saw that he was different. I had been ignoring all of the signs.

Now I was face to face with Regal's way of being in the world. He was not like the other kids, and I was afraid. I didn't tell Henry what I saw that day. I just talked to the teacher and told her that Regal was an only child and that he needed to spend time with other kids to accelerate his development. She assured me that she had had many kids in the same situation, and that he would catch up. But I knew it wasn't true. I knew something was up. But I wanted to believe that, so I did. Have you ever convinced yourself of something you knew was not true? It seems easier to believe the lie. But the truth makes you free, even when it hurts. But I wasn't ready for the truth. I was afraid. I didn't know what I was afraid of; I just knew I was afraid. So I kept ignoring the signs, hoping that preschool would be the magic formula for Regal to start talking and wanting to engage with other people. It seemed like a reasonable plan.

Meanwhile, it was hard to *unsee* what I had seen at preschool. Now I was paying closer attention to Regal's behaviors. It wasn't just the kids; he was not engaging with us either. He wasn't looking at us. He would run away laughing to himself when we tried to hug him. He played with toys differently. He lined them up. He had a sing-songy, nonsensical language. He walked on his toes. All of a sudden, I was noticing all of these things about my perfect son. But I "ignored" them. The plan was to let the preschool work its magic. Everything would work out. But would it?

## Kicked Out of Preschool

We got a call from the director of the preschool to meet with us two weeks after Regal had started. In my heart, I knew that it was not a normal, progress report meeting. Henry and I sat in those small chairs, listening to the teacher report on all of the things he could not do.

- Sits blankly in a corner and refuses to come out and engage with anyone.
- Refuses to communicate wants, needs, and ideas.
- Fails to have a conversation with a friend or adult.
- Disobeys classroom rules.
- Refuses to share toys or materials.
- Fails to cooperate with peers.

- Maintains eye contact with peers and teachers only rarely.
- Fails to participate in group learning activities.
- Fails to take turns in activities or games.

Reading these items was disheartening to say the least. It wasn't my son; it was a list of things that he couldn't do. Then to add insult to injury, they gave us a full refund, told us he could no longer continue in the program, and recommended that Regal be evaluated for developmental delays. My "preschool will fix Regal" plan was not going to work. I had come face to face with the truth. I had a choice. Would I deal with it or continue to ignore it? I sat there numb. I felt the room closing in on me. Their words were just words. I was not comprehending anything. My husband thanked them for their time, lovingly took my hand, and we made our way home. I had once again received an invitation to know the truth about Regal.

As I said previously, knowing the truth makes you free. From the moment I realized that Regal was different, I chose to ignore it. I chose to suppress it. This was my way of coping, but it didn't bring freedom. I began to see so many other things about him. Truth was leading me to freedom, even though I was not ready for it. There were so many things that were being highlighted about Regal. I chose to ignore them, but it did not stop them from being apparent. We were created to be in alignment with truth. It is our anchor. When we operate differently, it moves us away from being grounded. It ushers in uncertainty, doubt, and shame. I was seeing all of these things about Regal, yet I would ignore them and try to justify them. This in turn caused me to feel a lot of uncertainty. I found myself growing a lot more fearful. Has this ever happened in your life? When you ignore the truth, it diminishes your power. You spend your energy attempting to manipulate your life instead of owning it.

Truth says that I can face whatever is in front of me, with a confidence that I have faith, hope, and love to get through it—similar to when I had Regal and realized that I had the tools already inside of me to be his mom. Now, I was moving away from this in my state of feigned ignorance. But truth is very patient. It gently leads you—highlighting, revealing, and nudging— giving you an opportunity to own what is happening so that you can recognize the power that you have been given inside of you. Funny thing is, you don't always realize that's what's happening at the time. At least I didn't. That's why getting kicked out of preschool was the best thing that could've happened. It forced me to deal with the truth. But there was no way I could have prepared for what would happen next.

## Autism??

I called the Early Intervention Unit, and a three-person team was scheduled to do the evaluation. They asked all kinds of questions about our family. They wanted to know what our resources and strengths were. They asked us to share our concerns and priorities for Regal. The written assessment had happy little bear cubs all over it, and the questions were in the 1st person as if Regal himself was talking. It was extremely family-friendly. Any discomfort and hesitancy I had prior to the evaluation were quickly dismissed.

I shared his love for details, books, and music. I explained how he would examine a toy for hours but never actually play with it. I shared how inflexible he could be, and the meltdowns that occurred when our schedule had interruptions or changes. I was becoming more and more aware of his challenges as I answered each question. They made me think and focus realistically on Regal's way of being and his lack of language. The team then tried to play with him, and Regal didn't acknowledge their presence. He wouldn't even look at them. When they finished the evaluation, they immediately discussed the findings with us. There was no waiting period. It was time for truth to speak, and I was ready to hear.

There was a sixteen-page handwritten document that detailed Regal's results. They confirmed a delay of at least 25% in multiple areas of Regal's development, which meant that although he was 33 months old at the time, his development was closer to that of a 14 to 20-month-old. However, they could not give him a diagnosis, and recommended that we make an appointment with a developmental pediatrician for further testing. In the interim, they would begin services immediately in our home in order to help him become more interactive and attentive to people around him and their activities. We discussed the goal of helping Regal become more purposeful and functional with his words, so that he could get his wants and needs met and participate in simple conversations. They also recommended exploring Regal's processing abilities and the impact on his interactiveness and attention so that he could participate in preschool effectively. As we discussed his play, I learned that being more purposeful with his play, would facilitate growth in his cognitive skills.

As I listened to the results, I realized that if I continued to deny the truth, and protect myself, I would be leaving my son to fend for himself. I was leaving him unprotected. I was not helping him; I was hurting him by ignoring the truth. Love protects. It was time for me to move in love, and learn how to help my son. It was time for me to take a stand for my son.

The team and I worked on specific goals for Regal, based on their recommendations. As they solicited my input, I began to reclaim my power with each goal that I articulated. I wanted Regal to be able to say his name. I wanted Regal to answer questions about himself and the world as he saw it. I wanted Regal to tell us what he wanted, when he was hungry or tired or happy. I wanted Regal to play with his toys instead of examining them, and to be able to play with other children should the opportunity arise. The more I talked about what I wanted, the clearer my vision for my son became. When I do transformation work with women, clarifying what you want is a foundational principle. Vision is a life-giving, empowering force. It moves forward. It strengthens and builds up. When you focus on what you want instead of fretting over what you don't want, you are putting your stakes in the ground. This equips you for the journey ahead. I wasn't sure what was coming, but I knew that I would be able to withstand it. And it's a good thing too, because there were so many growth opportunities ahead.

## I Can't Stop Crying

We had made our appointment with the developmental pediatrician. It took almost a year to get on his calendar. Regal was given the diagnosis of Pervasive Developmental Disorder (PDD-NOS). He said that PDD refers to a myriad of conditions that involve delays in the development of many basic skills. The most common ones are demonstrated in a child's inability to socialize with others, to communicate, and to use imagination. He further explained that children with these conditions are also confused in their thinking, and generally have problems understanding the world around them.

PDD-NOS is no longer used in the DSM-5. It was one of the subtypes that has been folded to the overall diagnosis of Autism Spectrum Disorder. Regal had autism. The truth was on full display, and I was acknowledging it. I was moving forward in love to make sure that my son reached his full potential. I was walking in freedom and was committed to learning and growing. But why couldn't I stop crying? Every day I cried. I cried because I felt guilty for not listening to Henry. I cried because I was anxious about all of the work ahead. I cried because now I had to get used to having the Early Intervention team in my home. I cried because I did not have time to myself. I cried because a few months before Regal was evaluated, I had my daughter, Nia, and I was just exhausted. I cried because I was concerned about Regal taking all of the attention, and that I would miss something with, Nia. I cried because although I admitted the truth, I didn't feel free. I cried because I didn't feel warm and fuzzy when I was with Regal. I cried, I cried, and I cried.

Instead of suppressing my emotions, I owned them. I cried freely. I talked about what was happening, with my husband, my best friend, Cheryl, and my good girlfriend, Candyce. I was honest and authentic, and this strengthened me. It enabled me to stand in my power. When I teach women to access their inner resources, tears are at the top of the list. We've given tears a bad rap. I'm not sure who told us that it was weak to cry. Tears are one of our greatest resources. Tears were given to us for a reason. Research has shown that tears release toxins and stress. Did you know that when you cry, your tears have stress hormones and chemicals? Crying reduces the levels of these chemicals in the body. This reduces stress. Tears serve a purpose. Jesus, one of the greatest faith leaders in history, wept. The scriptures also talk about the tears that are stored in a bottle in heaven. They are precious. Even if you are not religious, you can appreciate the value of tears.

I was also mourning. Once I acknowledged Regal's diagnosis, I had to grieve the loss of my idea of having a typical child. And it was important that I took the time to process this, because I did not want to blame autism for my unhappiness. Grief and mourning take you beyond your initial reaction to a loss. It moves you to a place where you can live with loss in a healthy way. My tears were purposeful. I had to respect the process and honor grief. If you are currently in this place, here are some suggestions for participating in the process.

- Take your time. Don't allow anyone to rush you through your grief. Allow yourself to feel the sadness. Embrace it with the knowledge that it will pass.
- Lean on a trusted friend, someone who will sit with you and cry.
- Remember that this is a messy process. You will go in and out of grief. Be patient with yourself, and know that you will gain the strength needed to love your child.

I did not want to spend too much time grieving, because I recognized that Regal still needed me. But a process is a process. If you would like more self-reflection questions to guide you in your process, please visit helloautismbook.com/bonuses. This process was preparing me to love Regal well. I just didn't think it would be like this.

## Takeaways

# Chapter Two

# Why Is This Happening to Me?

*"If I were to say, 'God, why me?' about the bad things,*
*then I should have said, 'God, why me?'*
*about the good things that happened in my life."*
**– Arthur Ashe**

## I Can't Believe Regal Has Autism

Accepting the diagnosis was taking longer than I thought it would. As a faith leader and transformation coach, I expected more from myself. Why wasn't my faith pulling me out of this hole? What happened to mindset strategies and standing in your power? I was depressed. I wasn't weeping every day anymore; I was just sad. And I was angry. There was one question that was stuck in my head: "Why did this have to happen to me?" I was hung up on the *why* and *me.* Why me?

Questions are powerful. When you are asked a question, whether you know the answer or not, it's the only thing you can think about. You will either respond positively and search for the answer, or respond in fear and be paralyzed over giving the right answer. Either way the only thing you are thinking about is answering the question. Scientists call this *instinctive elaboration.* A question demands an answer. When you take the time to ask yourself important questions, you gain a better understanding of yourself. The questions will haunt you and move you towards seeking the answers that you need. I did not realize it at the time, but asking questions was a good thing for me to do. Even if I didn't get the answer.

"I can't believe Regal has autism" really meant "Why did this have to happen to me?" What exactly was "this?" "This" came down to admitting that I felt ill equipped to parent a child with autism. We had been receiving in-home Early Intervention services for about four months. They came to an end when Regal turned 3. When they first started, I was hopeful that Regal would experience dramatic results. There was some improvement, but it was not dramatic. Regal was able to say a few more words, and point to what he wanted. Now the in-home services were done, and Regal was placed in a special preschool, run by the Early Intervention Unit. The class was designed specifically for special needs kids. Not all of them had autism, but they each had their specific needs. The staff was loving and kind, and they were committed to the children.

However, I noticed that Regal began to imitate some of the behaviors that the other kids had. He started coming home and doing things he had not done before. I wasn't sure what could be done. I couldn't ask the teacher to keep Regal away from the other kids. She certainly could not try to stop the other kids. I did not expect that. But it really bothered me because I felt like he was going to school to learn how to diminish his behaviors, not pick more up. Let me pause and say that my understanding of Regal's behaviors were limited at this time. Had I known at the time that his behaviors were his coping mechanisms, I would never have tried to stop him. But you don't know what you don't know. And I was overwhelmed now, by the addition of new repetitive behavior patterns.

## Despair and Disappointment

I became disappointed with the school setting, not with the staff; as I said before, they were extremely dedicated to the kids. I just wasn't sure if the changes I was looking for would be accomplished in a classroom with so many competing needs. But I wasn't exactly sure what to do. More questions flooded my mind. What can I do? I am not qualified. Still no answers. However, I was not looking for answers. I spent my days with my questions in my head, which did not lend themselves to an answer. I had not engaged in asking other questions that would move me forward. It was pretty much a pity party. Why me? But again, this is necessary. It's like in the ancient wisdom literature songs of the bible: The writer spends the first half asking questions. Why me? Where are you? Why have you forsaken me? It is called a *lament*. Lament is a way to process the grief that comes into your life.

- It gives you language for your loss.
- It shields you from disconnecting with God.
- It gives you a place to bring your complaints.
* It is a process for your pain that reminds you that this is a journey.

There are a lot of benefits in lamenting. Lamenting helps us to express our pain, with the hope that there is meaning and purpose in life.

In these ancient writings, you will often see a pivot in the second half of the lament. The songs take a turn. You hear words of hope, words of expectation, and statements of faith and confidence. It's almost as if it's a different person altogether. I had accepted the fact that my son had autism. However, I needed to allow myself to feel the despair and disappointment. I needed to lament. This empowered me to move forward. Eventually, I began to entertain other questions. What are other parents doing? How do they get through this? What can I do? More of these types of questions began to come up for me. The question of *why me* began to fade into obscurity. I began to remember my commitment to love. Love never gives up. It never loses faith. Love is always hopeful. Love endures through every circumstance. It was time to love. My son needed my love.

It was interesting that as I began to move towards these types of questions, the answers began to find their way to me. I received an invitation from Regal's school to attend a four-week training on a therapy called *Floor Time*. There are so many other treatment modalities available now, but years ago as I was searching, Floor Time was new...well, to me it was. It has actually been around since the 80s, so it wasn't new. But it piqued my interest, so I decided to give it a try. I learned practical strategies for how to play with Regal. It bolstered my confidence, and I committed to implementing the strategies at home for 60 minutes each day.

I enjoyed that time with Regal. It was meaningful, and I felt more connected to him. Having a set time, with a plan, relieved my angst, and I felt like I was doing something purposeful. I also saw the value in taking ownership. Up to this point, my mentality was depending on the professionals to fix Regal. I realized that I had to be proactive and intentional in discovering ways for my son to connect with us. This was also empowering.

I had developed a friendship with another special needs mom, when we were receiving Early Intervention Services. The occupational therapist connected us. She lived a few minutes away from me, and our sons were the same age. Maddie and I attended the Floor Time training together, and it was helpful to have another mom figuring it out with me. I was attempting to do too many things by myself. I needed community. Maddie was the first of many other moms with whom I would develop relationships. Not only were they great resources, they were a vital part of my support system.

The biggest blessing came from a suggestion from my good girlfriend, Candyce. She shared that she knew someone else who had a child with autism, and whatever program they used had enabled him to live a full life. I got her contact information and set up a time to speak with her. All of these events came to me after I cared for myself by honoring the process and then beginning to seek solutions.

Here is the lesson. In order to love our kids well, we have to love ourselves first. Taking time to cry, grieve, and lament ushered me into a place of powerful questioning. These questions led me to resources and people that would help Regal. Love had provided for me. It led me to discover myself. It led me to new questions with solutions. It reminded me that there was an endless supply of love available to me.

Eventually, my crying diminished from daily to weekly. I was able to celebrate continuing to move forward in the midst of the doubts, misgivings, and disagreements I was having with myself. As I moved through my tears, I reminded myself of what I wanted for Regal. I did this by going back to the goals that I set with the Early Intervention team. I reiterated what I wanted for Regal, in hopes that the feelings of strength and empowerment would return to me. I did not always feel strong, but I knew that this practice anchored me. It was a dance. It was not perfect, and it was messy, but I kept moving forward, learning the steps to this imperfect dance.

## Love and Fear

As I learned to dance, I had to watch the tendency to lean towards fear instead of love. Elizabeth Kubler Ross says,

*"There are only two emotions: love and fear. All positive emotions come from love, all negative emotions from fear. From love flows happiness, contentment, peace, and joy. From fear comes anger, hate, anxiety and guilt. It's true that there are only two primary emotions, love and fear. But it's more accurate to say that there is only love or fear, for we cannot feel these two emotions together, at exactly the same time. They're opposites. If we're in fear, we are not in a place of love. When we're in a place of love, we cannot be in a place of fear."* A key component of learning the dance was training myself to choose love over fear. There was plenty to be afraid of.

Regal was pretty much at a standstill. He hadn't made any great strides, but he hadn't regressed either. I continued to do Floor Time with him for 60 minutes a day. The time that we spent together was not perfect, but we were spending intentional time together. I kept trying to get him to play games with me, but he was not interested. He would wander off and begin to "play" in his own way. I spent most of the time cajoling and inviting him to come and play with me. I know I wasn't doing things the "right" way, but I consoled myself with the fact that I was doing something.

I followed up with Candyce's friend, Jen, to learn about the program she did with her son. It was a home program, The Son-Rise Program™, founded by parents, for parents. It focused on social skills, building a bridge from the child's world into ours. A big component was acceptance and love. The more I researched the program, the more I knew it was the right program for us. But I was afraid of the amount of time that was needed to be successful, and I was concerned about the cost. The thought of finally finding a program that I thought Regal would respond to, and failing or not having enough money, was disheartening. I was afraid. But if I allowed my fear to set up camp in my mind, it would keep me from moving forward.

It's important to remember that when you have been directed to a solution, the resources will follow. It made absolutely no sense for this information to come to me so that I could be tormented. That's not how love works. But that is exactly how fear works. Fear is a dream crusher. It paralyzes you and keeps you from giving and receiving love. If you are locked in fear, you block the path for love to flow freely from you to your child. It may take a while, but eventually you will find the path. It took me almost a year before I decided to take action. While I was in limbo, working through my fears, I was taking steps. I kept looking at the website and reading the testimonials. I requested their free information kit and scheduled an information call. I checked in with Jen a couple of more times, asking questions and getting clarification. Finally, I sat down one day and made a list of everything

I was afraid of. Then I looked at each of those fears and decided that they were not big enough to keep me from this opportunity.

Over the years, I have developed this strategy and have taught it to other women to overcome their fears. Inspired from my former pastor, Bishop Wilbur Jones, I call it the Displace and Replace System (D & R) system. It is a simple process that you can use to displace the paralyzing thoughts. You see, there are only two kinds of thoughts: "Stay Put" thoughts (these are the ones that hold you back) and "Move Forward" thoughts (these are the ones that move you forward). The D & R system helps to acknowledge and displace the thoughts that hold you back, and replace them with thoughts that move you forward.

If you find your fears getting in the way, take a piece of paper and divide it into two columns. Write a list of everything you are afraid of for your child. Sit down and write. Write until you can't write anymore. Look at the list. Evaluate each item on the list. Ask questions. Is this true? Do I really believe this? Do I want to hold on to this belief? Take time to go through each item, crossing the ones off the list that you don't believe. Then whatever is left on the other side, write another outcome for the fear. Some of the fears I listed were: "I don't have the time to run this program"; "I don't have the skill set to train, supervise, and recruit volunteers"; "This program is too expensive"; I'll never be able to afford it." My alternative outcomes were: "Jen did it, so why can't I?" "Thousands of ordinary parents have gone through this program, from all walks of life, and if they can do it, I certainly can do it"; "I have been leading and training groups throughout my career in Student Development, so I know how to build a team." I can ask them: "How do parents fund their programs?" "Are there scholarships?" "Is there a payment plan?" "Is this covered by insurance?" These questions are filled with possibility and hope. By the time you finish the exercise, you have a page full of possibilities and hope. You have solutions.

You may be saying to yourself, "I don't have time to implement a D&R system in my life. Who has time to write a full blown list when you have a special needs kid?" Create the time. Keep a pad and pencil in the bathroom so that you can write when you sit on the toilet. I do some of my best thinking in the bathroom. Or have a paper and pen at the side of your bed. Or write your list instead of scrolling through your social media feed, or binge watching on Hulu. What about putting a white erase board on your refrigerator? We have a chalkboard in our kitchen. You can create whatever you want. Even if you are not able to write a full blown list, just get started. You can do it incrementally. Isolate the one fear you have, and write another narrative for it. Focus on the new narrative. You can download an example of the D & R system at helloautismbook.com/bonuses.

It's important to remember that fear and love can't operate simultaneously. Pay attention to what you are feeling. If it's coming from a place of fear, shift towards love, and continue to ask questions and make statements that are in alignment with love.

I shifted my fear to love, and love empowered me to take action. Yes, it took a while, but even "a while" is relative. More importantly is, where did I arrive and what did I learn in the process? We decided to give the home therapy a try. It was the best decision I could have made.

## Awareness and Understanding

We began implementing the home program. It took everything: my time, my talents, my energy, my patience, my resources, my intellect, my inner wisdom, my love. It was the best of times; it was the worst of times. The program was run by us. We were trained, and then we recruited, trained, and supervised volunteers to help us facilitate the program. The volunteers worked 4–6 hours a week. We had a special room set up in our home where the program was run. It was called the playroom. Initially, we ran the program part time for

20–30 hours a week. Regal was four and still attending preschool for a half day; we worked with him after school. In the second year, we took him out of preschool, and we were full time, 40–50 hours a week, every day, even on holidays. The program was founded upon a fun, loving, non-judgmental approach. It dramatically changed my view of Regal and how I loved him and people in general.

There were a few guiding principles that began to ground me and guide me into loving more.

- Everyone is doing the best that they can.
- Your child's "odd" behaviors are just their way of taking care of themselves.
- Your child can't come into your world, so build a bridge into theirs.

These were instrumental in changing my perspective about my life with Regal. I had been looking through the lens of "What's wrong with Regal?" "Why does he do those things?" "Why does he run away when I try to hug him?" Intellectually, I knew he couldn't help it, but my heart longed for connection. Having this framework gave me a path to understanding and awareness. This allowed me to let go of my judgements about Regal, and opened me up to give more love.

Once we began our program, my whole approach changed. When Regal would run around in circles talking to his hand, I celebrated his wisdom in taking care of himself. When I was changing his massive four-year-old poop diaper, I whispered to myself, "He is doing the best that he can." When he ran away from me when I tried to hug him, I laughed and ran around with him, remembering: "Your child can't come into your world, so build a bridge into theirs."

If you are going to love your special child well, you must be willing to gain greater understanding and awareness. It was an integral part of my growth, confidence, and effectiveness in guiding Regal to become his best self.

## Takeaways

# Chapter Three

# There Is More

*"I prayed for twenty years but received no answer until I prayed with my legs."*
– Frederick Douglass

## Accept But Don't Accept

Life is a gift. We were all created for a purpose. Every life has significant value. We all have been given a unique set of gifts and talents that are unique and specific to us. They are not always visibly apparent. Sometimes it requires an excavation. You have to dig deep. It takes a minute to discover, but if you're looking for them, you will find them. Your special child is no different. Every single soul that is born into this world has a specific purpose that only they can fulfill. There are a particular set of people in the world that are waiting for your child. There are human beings that need to know your child. There are individuals that need to experience your child. There is someone that needs to know your child. There is a community that is waiting to engage with them. There is a purpose.

You have to understand that someone's life will be enhanced by being in proximity with your special child. This is valuable information for you as a parent. Because if you're like me, you've put a lot of energy worrying that your child won't be accepted. You worry about how they will be perceived. You wonder what people are thinking. You apologize for their behaviors. I want you to realize that your child has a purpose that is connected to someone else. I'm not saying that you understand the purpose. It won't always be glaringly obvious, especially in the beginning. But it's important to believe there is a purpose.

When you operate from this mindset, you can accept the diagnosis but not accept the limitations of the diagnosis. Yes, Regal had autism. I accepted that. But what I would not do was believe that autism had the power to limit his potential. His purpose is greater than autism. If you want to love your child, you have to embrace this mindset. Your child's purpose is greater than their diagnosis. This will keep you moving towards love and away from fear. Love will energize you and ground you. It will keep you hopeful and expectant. Say that aloud: "My child's purpose is greater than __________ (insert diagnosis)." Their life is much more than the label that has been placed on them.

Life is more than what is seen on the outside. The essence of who we are is spirit. Spirit is invisible. If you focus only on what you see, you will miss the most powerful part of who you are. You must connect with the invisible part of your child—their essence, their spirit, their place of love. It is the most powerful part. Love will always respond to love. This is transformational. Although you may not be able to see it initially, this love will bring out the best in your child. Not only that, you are modeling to them what it means to be a human being. As you do this, all of the invisible qualities that come from love will be cultivated and multiplied in your child. We've created an attractive card that you can carry around with you to remind you of this. You can download it at helloautismbook.com/bonuses.

What does this look like practically? We are creatures of habit. Most of us have been conditioned to live in fear rather than love. It takes intentional acts to recondition yourself to live in love. I train the women that I work with to write truthful statements that remind them to choose love in order to keep moving forward. I call them Forward Declarations. Because of our conditioning, love isn't always our first response. It's a choice. And since we've been conditioned to respond in fear, despite our best efforts, it's what comes up first. Choosing love is a process, and it takes practice. It starts with identifying the qualities of love. Patience, kindness, faithfulness, endurance, humility, respect, sacrifice, focus, intention, calm, protection, selflessness, persistence, hope, and confidence are just a few. Come up with your own list. Write a few statements that express these love qualities. The statements should be true for you. Make sure they are true. You won't believe it if it's not true. And you become what you believe. "I am a patient person" may not work for you when your child has not been able to attend school for months because it is not the right fit, and every alternative you've been offered does not feel good to you. You are frustrated and concerned. You're scared, and tired of waiting. "I am a patient person?" That may not work. "No. I want my child in school. Now!" What is true? You've endured. You've been persistent. You keep going. That is love. "I will keep going until I find the right fit. I am developing patience, and this will help me make the right decision for my child." See the difference. Observe how different you feel when you say them. As you practice this, it becomes more natural. You will begin to find yourself responding more in love and less in fear. For a free download of sample Forward Declarations, visit helloautismbook.com/bonuses.

## Choose to Believe

The more I practiced acceptance and believing "My child's purpose is greater than autism," the more natural it became to accept Regal. It sounds simple, and it is. Simple should not be confused with easy; however, simple makes things attainable. Love was becoming my default response, so that when he was with me, he would feel my love, not my fear. Let me explain. My daughter was born shortly after Regal was diagnosed. Our experience was totally different. We saw her developmental milestones in a whole new light. She smiled and laughed. She said thank you and please. She asked for hugs and kisses. We cuddled and easily read her nonverbals. I could see her eyes light up and dance. I could hear her voice intonation. As I gave her love, she was able to give it back in a way that was easily interpreted. This energized me. It increased my happiness. It filled me up and made me want to do more and give more, and to enjoy the moments with her and give more of myself to her.

But with Regal, I did not receive obvious feedback. I wondered. I questioned. I doubted. I began to entertain questions: questions about my abilities, questions about Regal's future, questions about his place in the world—questions about world peace and global warming...not really. But my point is, I would go from a simple interaction with my son, to a worst-case scenario. Choosing to believe in his purpose safeguarded me from this practice.

I was not waiting for a response from him. I carried my own internal response. Regal has a purpose. He has value. People need his value. I am living in love. This love is being communicated to him, and he is receiving it and being changed and transformed. He feels my love. He is being changed by my love. I was choosing to believe and, in doing so, it kept me in that moment with Regal, focused on my responsibility to love him well, and filled with faith that my love was making a difference even though he was immersed in his own world, and even when it seemed like he didn't know how to care. He was self-sufficient and was content in his own world. So having a vision for, and cultivating the invisible qualities of love, helps to sustain you through what's visible.

## Searching for Answers

So you see how powerful love is? It gives you hope and vision. It opens you up to possibilities. Fear is the opposite. It keeps you focusing on the worst possible scenarios. It blinds you and prevents you from envisioning a bright future. This is why it is imperative that you do everything in your power to live in love. If not, you will not look for the answers. Each decision to love builds upon another decision. If you believe your child has value and a purpose in life, then you will not accept any report that communicates the opposite. This will inspire and challenge you to move forward in loving your child in order that the unique purpose will be accomplished in your child's life. Loving in this way requires action. Laying a foundation of acceptance, and doing your Forward Declarations, are essential.

The next step is to move into action to help your child reach their full potential and fulfill their purpose. You have to ask questions. You have to search. Love looks at possibilities. What resources are available to me in order to assist me in helping my child fulfill their purpose? Fear does not believe you are worth it or that there are options, and it causes you to settle. You can't just accept mediocre, less-than services. There has to be more for your child, because they have value and they have a purpose. What is available to you? You have to search it out, and it won't be easy. Many of the services that are available are not easy to find, are not publicized, or may be out of your budget. Find out what they are, and pursue them anyway! Because love takes a stand. You are standing for your child. Keep looking. Ask questions. Talk to other people. Join community groups. Facebook has a ton of them. There are networks and organizations committed to partnering with you on your journey. We have compiled a list of resources for you at helloautismbook.com/bonuses. What you need is out there, but you have to search for it. Ask. Seek. Knock. This is why you have to keep refueling your heart with love—so that you will have the drive to keep searching.

When I started searching for Regal, it was overwhelming to say the least. Understanding the information that was out there, and knowing what to look for, was not obvious. Today, there are so many treatment options that I believe parents can get overwhelmed by the sheer number of choices. But I discovered that it is a scavenger hunt; each piece leads you to the next clue. When you find one thing, you begin to search that out. You talk to people, and a conversation will lead to the next thing. Research it. Talk to more people, and it will lead to the next thing. You will see the pattern. You will be directed every step of the way. You will. The thing that would get in my way was when I doubted and questioned. When I moved towards fear, it would always take me off the path. I got back on track by staying true to my mantra of Regal has purpose. He was placed on this earth to fulfill it. There are resources available for me to help him accomplish his purpose. I have to look and find them. But they will be revealed to me. I will be patient. See how love undergirds you in this process?

## Finding Solutions

As you search and then discover solutions, it's not a cut and dry process. I think I used the word *messy* before, but I'll say it again: This is a messy process. You may think you have found a solution, and it doesn't pan out. It may be a therapy, and you do all of the research, and then you discover that the provider is no longer in your area. Or you talk to a provider, and it looks like a great fit. You begin working with them and then something happens, and you discover you are not on the same page with them. They are not good for your child. You have to stop. You are disappointed, and you may have even lost some money. It's okay. Keep searching. Don't stay in that place of disappointment too long. It will move you back into fear. Remember to keep moving towards love. Let love anchor you.

I was excited about a place that was recommended to me from one of our service providers. They were not in our network so we had to pay out of pocket. They were giving us a series of exercises that would help to stimulate Regal's brain. One of the exercises was for Regal to crawl every day. But Regal would not crawl. I couldn't convince him to do it. He was not cooperating. At that point in his development, he could not keep still. He was a runner. He ran all day long, singing and talking to himself. When I told them we could not get him to crawl, they suggested putting painful objects in his shoes to make his feet hurt so that he would have to crawl. Insert shock emoji here. I was not having it. I was not going to manipulate him in order to crawl. It did not line up with my philosophy of loving Regal. It wasn't truthful. What message was being sent to him by hurting him to make him crawl? I politely declined and never returned. Don't get so desperate that you are settling. Desperation comes from a place of fear. You are not thinking clearly. Quiet yourself and go back to your qualities of love. If it does not line up with them, trust that the right fit will come to you. Be patient. You don't have to settle.

## The Right Fit

It's a bit of a Goldilocks journey: This therapy is too hard; this therapy is too soft, but this one is just right! You have to keep searching until you get the right fit for your child—emphasis on *your child*. Every child is different. This is not one size fits all. What works for one child may not work for yours. Many people have had good results with ABA, but I was not a fan. I kept searching until I found what felt right for my child. The right fit for us was the home program. Facilitating it in our home, with a team of volunteers and a few professionals, felt right. We threw ourselves into it. When you find the right fit, I recommend going all in and not getting distracted by other things. There are no magic formulas. Faith and patience always yield results. I knew one mom who started in the Son-Rise program with me. She didn't see results right away, and she found something else. "No problem. Find what works." But when the results did not come fast enough for her, she started to look for another program. "No problem. Find what works." She did that for a few months and then moved on to something else. "No problem. Find what works." And then she moved on to another program. "Ummm, Sis? Are you sure about this?" You see the pattern. She never gave any program time to yield results. She was hastily acting in fear. Love is patient. It takes time and effort. When you have your right fit, stick with it. Be patient and diligent. Take it one day at a time, and follow the steps. You will see results in time.

## Takeaways

# Chapter Four

# I Love You But I Don't Like You

*"If you don't like something, change it.*
*If you can't change it, change your attitude."*
– Maya Angelou

## Loving and Liking

Everyone talks about how much they love their child, but liking... that's a little different. Logically, it was easy to love Regal. He was mine. He came from me, created in love. He was my answer to prayer after I had miscarried my first child. I carried him for nine months. He grew inside of me. He was my gift, a being that had been entrusted to me, and I loved him. God had placed a deposit of love inside of me for him. He was my son, my man child. I loved him. Love is steady. It's unconditional. It's deep and abiding. But liking? Hmmm. Liking is different. Liking refers to one's taste, to their preferences. Fondness and warmness are wrapped up in liking. Liking is enjoyment. And I was not enjoying Regal. I didn't understand him. I couldn't relate to him. He did weird things. He had odd behaviors. He was different. His differences were uncomfortable for me. He had delays in his development. Those delays required extra work on my part. That was not enjoyable.

For instance, Regal was not potty trained until he was almost 5. I remember one day walking into his room and being arrested by the pungent aroma of his bowel movement. He had taken off his diaper and started finger painting the room with his feces. Yeah, that was not a good morning. Or there was the time when he took off his diaper and left a pile of poop in the corner—another shining moment. Or there was the time when he decided he didn't want me to change his diaper anymore, and ran away midway, leaving a trail of poop smears throughout the hallway. I certainly didn't like that, and I equated my distaste for this with him. So when I thought about having to change diapers for a four-year-old, I didn't like him.

I was uncomfortable with the way he ran around on his toes and talked to his hand in a language I couldn't understand, especially when he did this in public. It was embarrassing when people would approach him to have a well-meaning interaction, and he would run away laughing while talking to his hand. I didn't like that. I interpreted it as rude and that it was a reflection on my parenting. I didn't like him. I didn't like how loud he talked, always drawing attention to himself and his differences. I was self-conscious of this, especially being one of the few African Americans in a predominantly white neighborhood.

I didn't like when he had to have things done his way. Life is unpredictable. We can't always account for the changes that occur. Regal loved numbers. Anything with a number, he was drawn to. There are several overpasses in our community that have the yellow signs with the clearance. Regal loved driving under those bridges and seeing the clearance signs. We began to drive him around the neighborhood and let him see the signs. There was a time when there was construction and the road was closed. We were not able to go under that bridge. This resulted in a full blown melt down that took a while for him to recover. I didn't like that. I didn't like when we went to the park and he would spend all of his time playing with the wood chips while everyone around him was engaging on the playground equipment. Regal would sit in a pile of wood chips, inspecting them. I didn't like that when we went outside, he would get distracted by the letters and numbers on the license plates. We lived on a college campus and were surrounded by cars and parking lots. If I did not hold him tight, he would run away from me to look at the license plates, making it dangerous for us to leave the house. I did not like that.

I could continue, but you get the picture. And if you're really tracking with me, you may notice something else. My dislike was about my discomfort. It had nothing to do with Regal. This was about me. I felt restricted. I was embarrassed. I was annoyed. I thought I was missing out. I couldn't have a typical experience with my child. It was hard. It was difficult. It wasn't normal. It wasn't fair. I did not like it. I did not enjoy it. So I transferred those feelings to Regal.

This wasn't about Regal; it was about me—although the potty training was legit. I did not like the demands that were being placed on me as a result of having a special needs child. I had to take a long hard look at myself. I did feel a little guilty, because he was special needs. How could I not like my special needs son? The things he was doing weren't his fault. He actually couldn't do them. It wasn't like he was trying to get one over on me. He was doing the best that he could. If he could do better, he would do better. So how do I reconcile the things that I don't like? Or a better word is, *enjoy*. I didn't enjoy being with him because I was thinking so much about the work that it took, and the cost...the investment of time. I didn't enjoy him. What could I do?

What can you do? It's actually very simple. Although the application is messy (there's that word again) and hard at times, it's a simple principle. You go back to the phrase that was given to me. "Regal is doing the best that he can." If you genuinely believe that he is doing his best, then that is all that you can get. The disappointment that comes from unmet expectations can color our experiences. Why would I expect him to do something that he is not able to do?

But the feelings are valid. In relationships, there are always going to be aspects that we don't enjoy. There are just things that we don't like about the people we love. I've been married for over 20 years. I love my husband. But I don't like everything about him. However, I enjoy the life that we have together. I don't focus on the things about him that I don't like. And I don't try to change him. The same is true for our children. It is possible to enjoy them. I wanted to enjoy Regal. I knew it wasn't realistic to enjoy every moment, but I wanted to enjoy my life, not resent it. In order to accomplish this, I began to change my focus. I couldn't ignore the difficult aspects—they were real—but I could choose how I responded to them. While I was cleaning the poop, I began to sing a song about poop. I made up a whole crazy, silly song about Regal and his poop. It was hilarious. It changed my energy and shifted me from being angry to laughing at myself. When he was having a meltdown, I would remain calm and let him cry, recognizing that change is hard. It's hard for all of us. I stopped myself from the inner conversations that said "What's wrong with him?" I would just be with him in that moment and be his anchor as he processed the change.

Here's what it all boils down to: It is your choice. There are behaviors that you won't like, but there are so many other things that you can enjoy. How will you choose? It's up to you.

## Facing Fear

Fear is at the core of all of this. My lack of enjoyment comes from my fear of the future. Not being potty trained comes down to, "Will he be able to live independently?" Meltdowns translate to, "Will he ever be able to control his emotions? How will he make friends?" I had so many fears around what he could do. Who would he become? What does this mean? When you get stuck in the future, you can't enjoy the present. The only thing I have is the present. Think about it. Your future is dependent upon how you live in the present. The work that you do in this moment will impact the outcomes of your future. So how will it benefit your child if you continually fret over the future? There are moments right now, in the present that you can capitalize on that will massively impact your child's future. This also applies to the past. You can't go back. You can't change anything. Focus on the present moment. You may be asking what you should do when you are afraid for your child's future. Acknowledge it. It's real. Don't ignore it. Find another parent or someone who understands to talk to. Oftentimes, you just need a space to be heard, to be validated. You just need encouragement. And then you move forward. Really? Yes, really. The more you do this, the more natural it will become to engage in this process. You won't get rid of your fear. We are human. We have fear. But you will learn to recognize that fear is a part of you. But it does not make you. And you don't have to let it stop you from enjoying your child.

## Acceptance and Forgiveness

Just as you must learn to accept your child, it's important to learn to accept and forgive yourself. I had moments that were not so fine (and I still do). I remember when Regal was a baby; I tried to put him in the carrier thingy, and I didn't have it secured properly. He fell right through it and hit his head. (I don't even think I told my husband that happened—sorry babe.) Or there was the time when were at a church event. Regal was tired. So was I. I didn't feel like chasing him. We were in a safe, secure space. I let him run around, and he fell and chipped his tooth, and blood was everywhere. There was the time when I walked into the poop smelling room, angry and frustrated, and I yelled, "What the hell is wrong with you?" Of course, there was no response from Regal; he continued business as usual in his own world. Or the time when I was so tired that I put Regal in his room, locked the door, and left him there for a long time (I won't tell you how many hours). He is 18 now, so child services can't take him away from me for neglect.

We have stories as parents. We screw up on the regular. Whether it's intentional or unintentional, you will have your moments. Accept your humanity. Forgive yourself and move on. There is too much work to be done for your special child to get stuck in the guilt trap. You are doing the best that you can. You won't enjoy everything about your child. You won't always have the perfect response. You won't act in the best of ways. But just know that you are doing the best you can. Believe that, and keep choosing to enjoy your child.

## Takeaways

# Chapter Five

# A Different Mindset

*"You can't make decisions based on fear and the possibility of what might happen."*
– Michelle Obama

## What Were You Thinking?

Living in love, choosing to believe, facing fear, accepting but not accepting—all of these actions take work, time, and patience. But the most important thing to note is that it takes a different mindset. You will need to be very aware of your thoughts if you are going to be successful. The odds are against you. The professionals will give you the facts about your child. Most likely, the facts will be grim and dim. They will list a litany of limitations, track the areas where he is underperforming, and create sections dedicated to what is not working. Don't get me wrong; we need a base. We have to be able to start from somewhere. Progress will not be appreciated if you don't know where you came from. So it's important, but it is equally important to remember that these are just facts. It's data collected based on observations of where your child is in the moment they were observed. What they can't observe is the future. And this is where your mind comes in. Your mind must create its own report to accompany the one that was given to you. You have to take the information given and remember that it is just that: information. It does not in any way tell you who your child is. It is just reporting on what they are able to do at this moment. You are responsible for determining what you think he can accomplish in the future. So it's important that you use the reports as fuel for the future.

There will also be family members that will challenge your way of thinking. There were a few family members that we intentionally stayed away from because they would not be able to support us in the mindset we were developing. It wasn't malicious, and I know they were doing the best they could. But their words did not complement the mindset we were attempting to develop. It is the same thing with friends, and even church members and coworkers. Whoever is in your circle that does not support the new mindset you are developing in order to love your child well, limit the time you spend with them. Because what you think about your child will impact how you feel about your child. How you feel will impact your actions. Your actions will determine your results. So what you think, is really important. Pay attention to your thoughts. It's a process. It takes time. But it's so worth it.

## Committing to the Process

Loving and liking are very subjective. They are based on our feelings. If our feelings change, we are no longer in love or no longer enjoy a person. There is also another approach. It's called committing to loving, committing to liking, or rather enjoying. When you operate from a commitment, you are saying that regardless of how you feel, you will commit to loving. You will commit to enjoying. This is much harder because commitments are unwavering. We have a problem with committing in our society. We don't like to commit. We wait for the last minute. We keep our options open. We overcommit and end up failing to commit. Commitment is serious. It's deep. It's powerful. When you commit, you enter into a deeper level. You move from surface to sacred. Most parents have already made a commitment to love their kids. But I'm talking about committing on a granular level—taking your big commitment and breaking it down into the day-to-day so that it does not get lost.

When we decided to run our home program, I knew it would take a great deal of time and energy. I worked as a resident director at Eastern University. We lived on campus in the residence hall, with 200+ college students. Eastern is a loving community. The students were like our extended family. Many of them affectionately called me Mama T, which I didn't like, but once one student started calling me that, it just spread, and I accepted it. So I was embarking on running this program, while shepherding 18 to 22-year-olds, simultaneously keeping my marriage healthy—and did I mention I had also had a 2-year-old daughter?

I didn't want my daughter, Nia, to get the short end of the stick as far as quality time spent with me. There were many eager loving students that were willing to play with her. She was in daycare two days a week. I also had another friend who came weekly to spend time with her while I was working with Regal, but there is no substitution for mom. I scheduled intentional weekly Wednesday outings, and carved out blocks of time to spend with Nia. Oftentimes, I was exhausted, but I wanted to commit to loving Nia and spending quality time with her. There were times when I was tempted to cancel our outing. I told myself that I have spent every Wednesday with her and she knows I love her, and that it is okay if I miss this one. But I was committed to keeping my commitment. So even if I was tired, I kept our time together. Now, we may have spent it napping together, or rather her watching a video while I napped and cuddled (wink wink), but I did the best I could in those moments.

The day-to-day commitment says it's important for me to show my child that I love them by being present. So it helps to break down your commitment. Create a commitment statement that will remind you why you are committing, so it doesn't get lost. You can visit helloautismbook/bonuses to see examples of commitment statements.

## Renewing My Mind

Every day is a new day unlike the one before. It may seem like it's the same, but it's a day that you haven't seen before. It is unique and different. You will never see it again. It is an opportunity to do something different. Do it differently. Do it with love. Make a change. These changes begin with our daily acts of thinking. One of your first daily acts must be to renew your mind. Just as you have received a new day, you have to reset your mind. Your mind is like a computer. It needs to reboot. There is so much information flowing through its gates that it is necessary to renew it. Renewing the mind is recommitting to what you believe about your child. What you think about your child will determine your success. What you think about your ability to love your child will determine your success. Both of these have their starting point in the mind. Careful attention and effort must be put into renewing your mind every day. Commitment statements are extremely helpful in this process.

## Getting the Right Tools

You are only as good as your tools. When we started finding out the best ways to reach our son, diet was at the top of the list. We chose a probiotic rich diet called the Body Ecology Diet. This diet used a lot of fermented foods, food combining rules, certain types of meats, and cultured veggies. This was a long way from what I was accustomed to eating. I am a Brooklyn born and raised African American woman whose ancestry hails from the South and the Caribbean. I grew up eating fried chicken, collard greens, macaroni and cheese, curry goat, cuckoo, codfish cakes, and pigs' feet. And now I am in the kitchen learning how to culture young coconuts and cabbage. I am eating vegetables for breakfast, and choosing not to eat processed foods. Eating this way required an inordinate amount of preparation. I was always cutting, dicing, or mashing something. Prior to this, I had never purchased fresh garlic. Now it was a staple. I was cooking with garlic every day. I found that peeling the garlic was time consuming, and that's because I didn't know what I was doing. I went to a kitchen supply store to find a tool to help me cut garlic and vegetables. They sold me a garlic contraption and something to cut veggies. I don't know what it was called and I didn't care. I just needed it to work. My time was shortened significantly in the kitchen. I also purchased a really good set of Cutco knives from a former student. I still have those knives. Thanks, Ronna! It cut down my time in the kitchen tremendously. I just needed the right tools.

When you are on this journey, you have to have the right tools in place. It's not enough to read this book. Or any book. It will inspire you, but after you finish the book, you have to set up shop and make sure that you have the necessary tools. Be intentional in developing a set of tools that works for you. These are foundational before you can build. We often want to move to action and results without laying a solid foundation. Your strength comes from within. Take the time to lay a foundation.

Here are some of my tools. Try these or find your own.

Prayer – I believe that God is the creator and sustainer of all. His love empowers me and connects me to an unlimited supply of hope, faith, and love. If you are not spiritual or religious, find a source of inspiration that you can draw from.

Meditation – Being still and quieting myself teaches me to be present and drown out the negative voices that try to distract me.

Read – I read scripture. If the bible is not your thing, read something that will inspire you.

Forward Declarations – My words have incredible power. I use Forward Declarations to create a new mindset, and to build strength and vision for what is possible. They are all within my reach with my words.

Visualization – We think in pictures. I use my imagination to envision images that will support my mindset.

Journaling – Pour out your heart on the pages. Write your thoughts, fears, and dreams. Celebrate your wins. Give thanks for another day, another chance to learn, grow and believe. Draw, doodle, write poetry. Create space for clarity and expression. This practice is extremely anchoring for me.

## Putting a System in Place

Tools are great, but if I use them haphazardly, they don't benefit me. So I set about making sure that I do these things every day. It takes planning and being intentional. It takes a commitment. A system ensures that I am keeping my commitment to myself and to my child. This is love in action. I have trained myself to develop a daily routine. Having a child on the spectrum can become overwhelming. It is easy to get swept up in the enormity of the journey. When I do transformation work with women, guiding them in developing these inner practices is critical. I spend a great deal of time on this in my #HelloLife workshops and online programs because they are so important. They keep us grounded. I do my practices in the morning before everyone else is up. I tried evenings, but I wasn't as consistent. I would forget, get caught up in something else, or fall asleep because I was so exhausted by the end of the day. Remember, they are practices, so that means you do it over and over again, regularly, until it becomes your way. I practiced getting up early. I've experimented with various times over the years, and I trained myself to make 5 am my sweet spot. Yeah, 5 am. What works for you is the best time. Whatever time you choose, commit to it no matter what. Find what works for you, and stick to it.

## Takeaways

# Chapter Six

# Learning to Love

*"Love is like a beautiful flower which I may not touch, but whose fragrance makes the garden a place of delight just the same."*
– Helen Keller

## Patience is a Process

You have the tools, you have a system, and you are practicing these things—and everything should just fall into place, right? Wrong! I want to emphasize that this is a process—a lifelong process. Remember, this is a love journey. Please give yourself permission to fall down, get up, take one step forward, take three steps backward, stop and catch your breath, quit, and then start again—and everything else in between. Growth is not linear. The course that you are running does not go smoothly from one step to the next. It is full of hills, valleys, bumps, lumps, potholes, sidewalk cracks, puddles...there's a lot of stuff that you will encounter. Patience is what you will inherit as a result of this process. We are not used to being patient in our culture. We can get pretty much anything we want in real time. When it comes to growing in love, and learning invaluable lessons, those take time.

I recently read an article about patience. It listed four science based benefits for developing patience:

- Patient people enjoy better mental health.
- Patient people are better friends and neighbors.
- Patience helps us achieve our goals.
- Patience is linked to good health.

It doesn't take a vision quest or solitude retreat to cultivate patience. Those are curated experiences to guide you on the journey. You have the gift of your special child. As you commit to loving your child well, patience will be cultivated in you. You and everyone around you reaps the benefits. Every day is an opportunity to develop this gift. Consider some of my gift moments:

- Carefully planning meals for the week, shopping, and cooking, only to have Regal push the plate away and refuse to eat.
- Listening to Regal say the same phrase over and over again to himself for at least 3 hours straight.
- Being unable to sit down as a family and eat dinner.
- Realizing there are no more shirts for Regal to wear because he has chewed through every single one.
- Letting Regal stand at the entrance of the grocery store and watch the automatic doors open and close until you absolutely have to leave for the next appointment.
- Letting Regal take his time and look at every single price on the shelf in the grocery aisle because it brings him sheer joy every time he announces the number.
- Listening to Regal sing the potty song, "Yes, I'm going to the potty potty," all day long, even though he still is not going to the potty.

Patience is being cultivated. Seeds are planted in order to bring forth a greater harvest. Practice patience in your everyday situations with your child. You are giving yourself a gift that spills over into every area of your life. So when you find yourself in a gift moment, smile and say, "Thank you, Patience."

## Seven Words

There are seven words that help you to be more patient and loving with your child. I remember that after we had been running our program for a few years, Regal was making enormous strides. He was talking and making eye contact. We were having conversation loops and playing games together. It was not as much of a struggle to leave the house. He was not as prone to run away from us to examine numbers or letters. We were enjoying the fruit of our labor. We decided to take our first family vacation. It was a big event. We had never been able to take a vacation. We went to the Poconos, and we had a 2-bedroom apartment, thanks to my parents' timeshare.

When we got there, he ran around the apartment turning all the lights off and on. He opened and closed every door in the apartment. We laughed and let him roam and check everything out. He went to the microwave in the kitchen, pushing the numbers. We didn't have a microwave at home. Our home was electronic free. We intentionally removed all electronics that would be a distraction to Regal engaging with us in our home. So I immediately unplugged the microwave.

The first day, we had a great time together as a family. The kids played in the Jacuzzi, and we played some games together. It was wonderful. The next day, we planned to go out for a walk. Regal did not want to leave the apartment. He wouldn't leave. He refused to leave. I was disappointed. I wanted us to continue doing things as a family on our first vacation. But Regal would not leave. Instead of allowing disappointment to seep in, I recognized that Regal was doing the best that he could. Henry took Nia out for a fun daddy and daughter day, and Regal and I stayed together. We had a lovely day and great family time when Henry and Nia returned. I was able to shift my mindset because of these seven words: "Regal is doing the best he can."

What are you trying to make happen, and it is just not going the way you would like? What are you trying to force your child to do? What thoughts are keeping you up at night? Remember this sentence: "__________ (insert your child's name) is doing the best they can." Let patience work its course. All will be well. Remember they are doing their best, and return to loving them well. You can get a printable reminder to carry with you or post in your home, at helloautismbook.com/bonuses.

## Wake Up and Pay Attention

*Sister Act* is one of my favorite movies. There's a song in one of the scenes: "If you wanna be somebody, if you wanna go somewhere, you better wake up and pay attention."

Learning to pay attention to Regal was ongoing. Oftentimes I needed to make adjustments. As Regal began to grow and respond to the work we were doing with him, I realized I was becoming focused on solving problems. I was missing out on Regal. There was always one more thing in my head that I was wondering about. I would be thinking about a new therapy, wondering about the supplements and if they were working, and figuring out how to raise funds so that we could implement a treatment that wasn't covered by insurance. I was thinking about creating goals for Regal but not celebrating the attainment of his present goals. I was thinking about our volunteer team, and how I could best develop them so that they would continue to be effective with Regal. I was thinking about recruiting new volunteers, planning the menu, and cooking new foods and wondering how I could make it attractive enough for him to eat it. The list goes on and on. I was not paying attention to Regal. I was paying more attention to the details that involved Regal. It was brought to my attention by one of the program instructors with which I did monthly dialogues. I knew she was right. But I needed to do these things so that Regal would keep developing. I couldn't slow down for one minute. What was I supposed to do?

## Trusting Myself

She asked me, "What do you believe about Regal's progress?" "How did he get there?" "What matters most?" This was to help me realize the answers, and it came back to one thing: trust. I had stopped trusting myself. I was getting results, but I was beginning to become fearful that the results would go away if I did not stay on top of things. I had forgotten what had brought us to this place. I had to trust myself and the love that was guiding me. God is love. His love never leaves us. Why would it stop? I was focusing on what I could see. I recommitted to the invisible, trusting the love that guided me, and knowing that this love would continue to lead me to each step. I didn't have to drive myself. I did not have to try to force the results. Growth is the byproduct of love. Everything love touches grows. That's what I was supposed to do: trust myself and the love that guided me to each step.

When you find yourself going down this path, ask yourself, "What do you believe? How did you get there? What matters most?" Trust yourself. Trust that love will lead you. You can never lose love. All will be well.

## Takeaways

# Chapter Seven

# One Day at a Time

*"Instead of looking at the past, I put myself ahead twenty years and try to look at what I need to do now in order to get there then."*
– Diana Ross

## Endurance Training

As I continued on the journey, things that used to be so difficult became second nature. Questions that I had, no longer needed answers. Discomfort that I felt around Regal's differences were no longer an issue. I had grown accustomed to my way of life. It was my new normal. I was discovering a power and a strength that I did not know I possessed. Do me a favor, right now. I want you to imagine that I am standing in front of you, smiling and lovingly putting my hands firmly on your shoulders. Can you see me? Now, hear me: You are stronger than you think. You can carry more than you realize. You have the capacity for endurance. Trust me. You do. However, your strength will never be realized unless you continue on the journey. You are a person with unlimited potential. It is not discovered in times of comfort, ease, and satisfaction. The growth is born out of the struggle. There must be agitation. There must be friction. There has to be some type of resistance in order for the best parts of you to be seen. We discover who we are when we are in our most difficult moments.

If that is true, why don't we embrace these moments? Why not run towards them? We don't like pain. We don't like discomfort. We avoid it at all costs, and our mind supports this. The mind's job is to protect us. The mind's job is to help us survive. When it sees something that looks like a threat to our comfort, it goes to work to pull us out of that situation. So we tell ourselves stories that keep us from leaning into the pain. We stop short of the finish line, missing the opportunity for growth. Growth comes in the struggle. You have to overcome the barrier of pain in order to experience the pleasure—the sweet victory—and the joy and blessing that accompanies the victory. But it frequently takes time to get there.

This is really about endurance—staying the course regardless of difficult or unpleasant situations and processes. Refuse to give up. Steel is being formed inside of you. Steel is made by mining the iron ore and then taking it through a process, which involves heating and melting in blast furnaces in order to remove impurities, and then adding carbon to make steel. Our journey with our child extracts the substantive stuff from beneath the surface, removing the impurities through the furnace of parenting a special needs child, and adding more faith, love, hope, wisdom, patience, and experience to produce a stronger, effective, and useful person.

Your child is also going through their own process. They need you to bring out and reveal what is there. It is there waiting to be seen and used for the benefit of someone, and it takes time to draw it out. As you engage in this process with your child, little things that we take for granted become victories. Traversing this love journey with your child makes you an expert celebrator. We became very good at celebrations; every day had the potential to be a party.

Whenever Regal looked at us, we celebrated his eye contact. When he asked for something using his words, we celebrated. When he stayed engaged for longer amounts of time, we celebrated that. We celebrated the big things too, like when he started using the potty at age 5 (thank God), and when he learned how to ride a bike at age 9. We celebrated when he was able to tie his shoes at age 9. We celebrated when he could eat collard greens, in their natural state, at age 10 (prior to that, I had been pureeing all of his veggies). We celebrated with him being able to blow his nose at age 13. These are everyday things that were major milestones in our world. Each one was worthy of a celebration, a dance party, a hip hip hooray.

I remember emailing one of Regal's therapists to share one of his victories. She responded so poignantly:

*"It amazes me how much most people take for granted, and how vulnerable we all really are. Sharing the load and the road is what really returns us to our humanity. Regal is a very lucky boy to have you for his mother, and you are blessed to have him to show you realms and depths you may not have experienced otherwise. There will be many victories to celebrate, and that is one of the benefits of having special needs—the things that others take for granted are cause to celebrate, and the celebration can be so much fun!" ~Judith Bluestone, Founder of The HANDLE Institute*

Celebrate the process. Celebrate your victories with your child. Nothing is too small. Tasting a new food, getting a haircut, saying hello, shaking someone's hand, making a request, pointing, smiling, being willing to do something new, sitting still and smiling for a picture...add your own to this list. Celebrate!

## Ask for Help

Many people have difficulty asking for help. I've been there. We've been taught in our society to help ourselves. Figure it out. Be strong. Be independent. It takes strength to admit when you are overwhelmed and need assistance. It's okay to call for backup. It's healthy to reach out. Too often, we delay asking, and stalling only leads to our demise. A manageable situation quickly escalates to unmanageable, all because we did not ask for help. There are a myriad of reasons why we don't ask. Fear, pride, shame, to name a few...but please consider this: It's not about you. There are people that have solutions for what you seek for your child. You can work through your feelings later. Don't let them stop you from getting what you need for your child and, ultimately, yourself. You are not helping yourself by attempting to figure it out on your own. You tried it. It ain't working. Ask for help.

One of the easiest ways to get help is to join a support group. When our son was little, we used yahoo message boards. Today, there are several community fb groups at your disposal. There are also parent support groups and networks that are available through various organizations. Talk to your doctor; they are also great resources. Family members and friends may want to help but are not sure what they can do. Take some time to think about where you need help. Child care? Finances? Household chores? Encouragement? Time?

When we got Regal's diagnosis and decided to run a home program, we sent a letter to all of our family, friends, church members, and colleagues. It was a support letter. The purpose was to raise awareness of what we were going through, what we needed, and to invite the people that loved us to participate. It was a bold move. We made ourselves vulnerable. But the response was amazing. We outlined our plan. We told them what we needed. We gave specific ways they could help. They could give time to watch my daughter while I worked with Regal, time in helping me with little things around the house, and prayer and words of encouragement. They could give financially towards the funding of the home program, or anything else they came up with.

To date, the response to our support letter has been the most amazing and humbling thing I have ever experienced. People gave their time, talents, prayers, encouragement, and money —all because I took a risk and asked for help. What you need has already been provided for you. You just have to ask for it. If you'd like to see a copy of our letter, go to helloautismbook.com/bonuses. Feel free to use it as a template to ask for help.

## Build a Community

Sending the letter helped to build a community. I needed this community. One of the most important aspects was that they not only supported me, which was huge, but they kept me accountable. Knowing that these people were giving themselves to our son so generously, kept me from having a pity party. I was filled with gratitude. I felt a responsibility to make sure that I was doing everything on my part. I had to keep going. I had to keep investing in Regal. I had to keep taking care of myself. They believed in me. They believed in my family. They believed in the work that Henry and I were doing. When I did not believe, I leaned into their belief. Their faith carried me on many an occasion. They kept me encouraged. I knew I was not alone, and I could not isolate myself because I had invited them in, and now I could not get rid of them. They were there constantly, checking in and inquiring how they could help. People were coming over in my space and in my face. I couldn't hide. I didn't always like it, I'm an introvert so having so many people in my home really stretched me, but it was what I needed. It pulled me out and kept me grounded. It kept directing and refocusing me to remember the work, our mission of love. I was watching the power of love on full display. This community was God's love personified. We needed each other.

You might be thinking that my situation was unique. "That doesn't happen with everyone." You're right. But not everyone asks for help. Not everyone is willing to allow people into their space. Not everyone will admit when they are weak and need support. If you ask for help, you will get help. I am grateful for my community. Granted, I did have a large community to draw from, because of my investment in people over the years. When I had a need, it was returned to me in the measure that I had given out over the years. So if you have not opened yourself up to other people in some way, it may be difficult at first. However, it is never too late.

## Keep the Faith

Faith carried me through it all. My faith is rooted in the Christian tradition. I believe that there is a God who reigns supreme over all. He is love, and everything he does is in love. His love is stronger than death, demonstrated by the crucifixion and resurrection of Jesus. This carries me, and I am anchored in the belief that God's love is stronger than death. Anything I face on this earth pales in comparison. My faith is bigger than me, so it does not crumble under the weight of the pressure that comes with the blessing of parenting a special needs child.

No matter what your faith tradition, you have to have a belief in something greater than yourself. Humans fail and waiver. Your faith must be greater than humanity. Whether you express it as God, the universe, higher power, or a spiritual force, it must transcend your abilities.

You must also have faith in your inherent value and the value of your child. As I said before, every soul has a purpose. Let your actions, decisions, and thoughts be guided by this, and never give up.

## Rinse and Repeat

The conclusion of the matter is this: Believe. Connect. Act. Keep doing these things over and over again. They are simple but in no way easy. But they are proven practical principles. Do them again and again and again.

For a list of autism support groups, visit helloautismbook.com/bonuses.

## Takeaways

# Chapter Eight

## Time Flies When You're Having Fun

*"I got my start by giving myself a start."*
– Madame CJ Walker

### Days Turn Into Months

"The days are long but the years go fast." Somebody said this to me when my kids were small. This could not be more true. At first, I was counting every minute of the day. It seemed like I could not get through one day without crying, or being afraid or feeling confused. I couldn't wait for Regal to go to sleep so that I wouldn't have to deal with the overwhelm of being with him and feeling disconnected. Or just waiting for the moment when I could finally fall asleep and not have to think about all of the details. But as the days continued, I began to figure things out. I started to connect the dots. I met other moms on the same path, and I began to grow in confidence. The days were no longer unbearable. That's what happens when your perspective changes. The days become opportunities. When you are looking through the lens of opportunity, you look with faith, expectation, and hope.

### Months Turns Into Years

My days were filled with three activities: believing the best, learning all that I could to continue to develop my son, and connecting with my community. Living with these guiding principles made every day an adventure... well, not every day, but most days were pretty adventurous.

I began to live with expectation. Things did not change. I had changed. Regal was still very much autistic. But I did not feel like his autism was a life sentence. I was no longer driven by fear and the litany of imitations. I was fueled by hope. I expected more for my son. What did I have to lose? What benefit is there to believing the worst case scenario? For all the realists out there, I was not oblivious to my son's diagnosis. I was choosing to believe that there was a way through it that would bring good to him and everyone that came in contact with him. I believed there was good. That alone shifted my perspective. When you believe that autism is a bad thing, it prevents you from living a full life. What is there to look forward to?

I was living with the mindset that my life was good with autism. Actually, many of the good things I was experiencing was because of autism. I was free to live a full life with my family and create my happiness. It wasn't based on the things I had; it was based on who I was. This was a game changer. The mindset work is ongoing and ever evolving. You never arrive; you have to keep doing the internal work. In my #HelloLife trainings, I've watched women transform their lives from learning mindset strategies. I've transformed my own life as I committed to persisting in this mindset. My belief that nothing is too difficult has taught me to live confidently. All things are possible, and the only limitations are the ones that I place on myself.

Running a home program, we were met with lots of challenges. But I viewed each challenge as an opportunity. Our program depended on recruiting volunteers. Every year, I had to believe that there would be people out there that would give their time to our program—college students at that. Each volunteer gave 4–6 hours a week. I leaned heavily on the Eastern University community. I went to club fairs, talked to professors and asked them to give extra credit, negotiated internship opportunities, and gave talks to student organizations. I posted fliers and sent emails. My enthusiasm was contagious. I discovered that people wanted to be a part of the miracle. They wanted to give. They wanted an opportunity to serve. They gladly gave their time. They were open to feedback. They wanted to grow. They wanted to develop themselves. They were grateful to be a part of the mission. They loved our family. They loved Regal. They were grateful for the opportunity. This wasn't a charity case. We had something to offer. Every year, without fail, I invited quality students to participate in our program; and every year, they accepted. They were loving, dedicated, and grateful for the opportunity to serve our family. I taught them how to connect with Regal. This taught me and made me a better person. These were the things that I was afraid of when I first contemplated the program, but now I was a recruiter, marketer, and trainer.

I patiently learned about nutrition and alternative therapies, taking my time to read through pages and pages of information, which is not my strength. I am more intuitive and rank high on emotional intelligence. Research does not light me up. But I took my time, digested the information in small bites, asked questions, and took breaks. And I kept at it till I found the doctors and therapists that had what my son needed, sometimes traveling 2–3 hours for a one- hour visit. Was it comfortable? No, quite the opposite. But I pushed through my discomfort to get what I needed for my son, because I believed that he had a purpose, and I was determined to find what I needed to help him reach his potential.

I became the advocate, ambassador, and champion for my son, in intimidating spaces, sitting in IEP meetings as the professionals throw around big words and acronyms. I was not sure who to trust, and was constantly questioning my ability. But I kept at it. And through my research and conversations, I learned that there are advocates that assist parents in IEP meetings. So I invested in an advocate. I didn't try to figure it out. I realized that I didn't have to do it all by myself.

I built a community around us. They were loving, supportive, and loyal. Not only did Regal reap the benefits, we all benefitted. We learned from each other. We grew as humans. We became better. Days turned into months. Months began to turn into years. My faith grew. I developed a skill set I didn't know I possessed. I no longer felt alone and, yes, I began to see changes in Regal.

## Ch-Ch-Changes

As I began to change internally, Regal began to change externally. It started slowly and began to pick up momentum. He began to look at us. His eye contact improved. He was more engaged, having more and more conversation loops. He was telling us what he wanted, expressing his opinions, and showing us who he was and his likes and dislikes. His confidence was growing, and he was taking risks. He was able to leave the house without meltdowns, and was becoming more flexible. He was showing an interest in people over objects. He was playing games, laughing at jokes, and initiating conversation. His personality was coming out. There was a twinkle in his eyes. He was showing us his mischievous side and doing things to get a response out of us. I remember when he first told a lie. We were thrilled.

Another milestone was when he came into the apartment after I had just finished making cookies. He said, "It smells like chocolate chip cookies, Mom." This was a huge moment because Regal could not identify smells. We had been diligently giving him different scents to smell, each day for years. Smell is closely linked to parts of the brain that process emotion and memory. His pronouncement that day let me know that it's working. Keep at it.

When we began to see changes, it was like they all started surfacing at the same time. It was crazy. Once he started growing, there was no stopping him. He was a force that could not be reckoned with. He started setting goals for himself, telling us what he would do.

Regal was on a mission. He had found the portal. There was no turning back.

## My New Normal

I felt so alive. I felt like I was a part of something bigger than me. I was raising awareness. I was living a life of love and acceptance, and teaching it to the volunteer team every day as they worked with Regal. Gratitude was being woven in the fabric of my soul. As I patiently waited for Regal (sometimes not so patiently) to emerge, I developed the practice of daily mind renewal. I had to keep doing the work and, at times, it was hard work, but it was wonderfully rewarding. I couldn't help but wonder what my life would have been like without autism. I was genuinely enjoying my life. I woke up every day choosing to be thankful, choosing to enjoy my son. I laughed freely and danced often. I was choosing freedom—freedom in my mind, freedom in my heart—a decision that freed my soul. Once I made the choice to love, it flowed to me, and everyone around me benefitted. It was always there. I just needed to make the choice. Love saved my life.

# Takeaways

# Chapter Nine

# Becoming a Student

*"Change will not come if we wait for some other person, or if we wait for some other time. We are the ones we've been waiting for. We are the change that we seek."*
– Barack Obama

## The 3 G's

I was an eager student. What was once onerous became my classroom. I had access to a plethora of master classes doing life with Regal. There were daily lessons to be gleaned from literally every aspect of my day. I was now open to the lessons. And I can't say enough about being open. I stopped fighting, resisting, defending, comparing, complaining, pitying, and all of the other "ing" superlatives. Three attributes made me undefeatable. I call them my 3 G's. They are gratitude, growth, and gumption.

There are tons of books devoted to gratitude, and for good reason. The practice of cultivating a grateful heart is the foundation. Gratitude is more than being grateful for what you have. It anchors and strengthens you. It moves you beyond yourself, and inspires you to give to someone else. Gratitude changes you. It creates a willingness to forgive; it softens your heart and brings healing. There are scientific benefits to gratitude, like an improvement in psychological health, reduced stress and anxiety, and improved self-esteem, empathy, and mental strength. There is improvement in physical health, like better sleep, lowered blood pressure, and reduced stress. I could give you statistics and case studies, but nothing can take the place of personal experience. I realized a noticeable change in myself as I lived in this place of gratitude. Your perception is your reality—good, bad, or indifferent. Your experience is your experience. The science helps to give language to what I was experiencing. My reality was that I felt good. I was happy. I was hopeful. I had energy. I was motivated. I was grateful. My life was hard. My days were long. I was often stretched and challenged. But it was not a burden. It did not deplete me; it added to my life. It was gratitude.

Growth is the result of gratitude. I was committed to growth. I remember being a young wife. We were in a couple's session, and I was not so open at the time. I did not realize it; I just thought I was right, and I was committed to being right. The therapist so skillfully stated, "Henry, you are open; you want to grow. Theresa does not want to grow, and you have to respect that." Hearing her words were like arrows to my heart. She wasn't even trying to change my perspective. She was actually challenging my husband to stop trying to change me and let me be who I am. But instead, hearing myself characterized as a person who did not want to grow, haunted me. "I do want to grow," I said.

We were created for expansion and fuller expression. Just look at the natural progression of all living things. Everything has a beginning. If it does not grow and flourish, it is not considered healthy. If you are not growing, you're dying. When you willingly participate in the growth process, your learning increases exponentially. The greatest gains are seen in our difficult places. The best stories are the ones that involve overcoming an obstacle, climbing a mountain, or walking through the fire. The best adventures are the unknown territories that we conquer to make it to the other side. As harrowing as these may be, there is energy, excitement, and enthusiasm that can accompany the experience. A healthy life is a life of growth.

Gumption is shrewd or spirited initiative and resourcefulness. I knew that no matter what I faced with Regal, we would figure it out. There was a way. Simply put, if you believe there is a way, there will always be a way. I kept my 3 G's close to my heart. I leaned into them, lived them out and—expected results. It wasn't optional. Results were already attained in my mind.

## Looking in the Mirror

One of the things we were taught in our home program was to allow Regal to have control. We would spend time in his playroom, teaching him how to play, building a bridge from his world into ours. Building the bridge meant that he couldn't come into our world, so we would go into his world. His world consisted of repetitious play. Regal loved numbers and letters. He would spend hours looking at these foam letters that we had. He would just lay on his back, hold a letter up, and inspect every single aspect of the letter. Prior to starting our home program, I would try to get him to spell a word or play with a different toy. I've even been guilty of taking the letters and giving him something else to play with, which by the way never worked.

Well, now we were giving him control and building a bridge, respecting him deeply, which kind of goes against my black mama default, where I would say, "Boy, gimme that letter. Come over here and play with this train." Once again, it doesn't work. We were taught to join him in whatever he was doing, and to join him wholeheartedly with all of the enthusiasm, excitement, and energy we could muster. So I would lay on my back with my own letter, and look at it the same way that Regal looked at it. Whatever he did, I would do. I wasn't imposing what I wanted on him. I let him take the lead. I followed whatever he was doing.

The response was amazing. It was like we were each other's mirror, only we weren't looking at each other. When I lay next to him and did what he did, he stopped and looked in my eyes. The first time he had ever looked at me. I went crazy with celebration. He smiled and went back to examining his letter. I did the same. This was how we played. It was deeply respectful, deeply child centered, and deeply profound. What happened was that the more I gave him control, the more willing he was to relinquish his control. We developed a trust and rapport with him. Eventually, on his own terms, at his own pace, he allowed me to introduce new ways of playing with the letters. He began to look at us for longer periods of time. He would allow me to change things up and play different games that were built upon his interest. It started from my willingness to see Regal's world and enter as the student, not the teacher.

## Letting Go

I was learning to surrender. There is power in surrendering. The more I relinquished my control, the more freedom I had with Regal. There is a serenity that accompanies surrender. I am no longer responsible for a particular outcome or result. I am 100% invested in learning from my child, studying, and appreciating him. He has something to teach me, so I will engage him in a way that communicates honor and respect, because I want to learn. We still set goals for Regal, and we were intentional in creating games that facilitated those goals. However, I let go of the timelines. I surrendered my ideas of when he should have these goals mastered. It taught me to be in the moment. I became less attached to an outcome, and more in the flow. This flow opened me up to more creativity, spontaneity, and imagination.

## Lessons From My Village

As I committed to learning, everyone became a teacher—Regal, the volunteers, my family, our community—everyone had something to teach me. And the lessons always returned me to love. I won't try to list every lesson. I will just sum it up in a few sentences. We were created to love and to be loved. The more love you receive, the more you want to give away. We were building a community of love, and everyone was being transformed. What started as a miracle mission for Regal, became an opportunity to demonstrate love and be transformed by love.

If you're still wondering what your child's purpose is, take this and build upon it. Your child was given to you to learn how to receive love and give love. This impacts everyone around you. Your child really is making the world a better place.

# Takeaways

# Chapter Ten

# A Whole New World

*"What's the world for if you can't make it up the way you want it?"*
– Toni Morrison

## A Different Lens

Every year, I go to the eye doctor. She makes me look through the machine with various lenses, and I have to tell her which combination allows me to see the best. It takes a few tries. We keep adapting, keep adjusting, and communicating until we arrive at the best fit for my eyes to be able to see clearly. This is what it takes to maintain a loving, liking, and learning state of mind. You have to keep adjusting, adapting, and communicating in order to see clearly.

Once you get your mind right and you begin to live a lifestyle of believing the best, refusing to settle, and facing fear, it can actually become monotonous and a little boring if you're not careful. When the excitement of developing a new skill wears off, you can become accustomed to it. The rush that comes with attempting to do something new, and accomplishing your goal, tempers off. It was said that Alexander the Great cried because he had no more worlds to conquer. The focus, intensity, and direction required for achieving a goal keeps you energized. You actually get a shot of motivation and happiness from your brain when you are anticipating an award. The brain releases dopamine, and that makes you feel good and want to keep going. When you accomplish your goal, the dopamine release drops, and it's harder to keep going.

It's important to keep doing the work. You have to keep doing the same things. Keep checking in with yourself. Keep adjusting your mindset. Keep listening to your child. Keep connecting with your community so that you can see clearly. Keep readjusting your goals so that you have something to keep working towards. I know it sounds crazy; with a special needs child, there is always something to work towards, but your vision can get blurry if you are not committed to these little things. You may begin to get confident and start letting little things slip.

When Regal expanded his pallet and started eating a variety of foods, I did not have to make as many adjustments, because he could eat more. At the same time, he was growing in his development, so we could go out more and visit new places. I started allowing him to eat some "good" processed foods. With holidays, vacations, and family gatherings, I was not as cautious and not as diligent. I couldn't understand why certain things were happening with Regal. They were little changes. He was not as focused, and he was a little more irritable and a little more energetic. They were subtle changes. I then realized that his diet had slowly swung to the left. I had to realign. Perhaps I would not have noticed if we were not tracking everything. I was able to course correct and readjust. Ancient wisdom says "It's the little foxes that spoil the vine." Beware or rather be aware. Stay focused. Stay diligent. Keep adjusting your vision so that you can see.

## Being Instead of Doing

It's also easy to get caught up in results when things start moving. Regal was moving at such an accelerated pace. I mentioned earlier, my tendency to get caught up in all of the things that needed to be done. This is tricky because there were a lot of things that needed to be done. We were having weekly team meetings, tracking his progress, and continually assessing and re-evaluating his goals.

When Nia started kindergarten, Regal was a part of it. He went with us to get school supplies. He listened to Nia talk about how much she was looking forward to going to school. He watched her get on the school bus every day. He went with us to visit the school. Regal met the teachers and visited the classroom. He saw Nia's desk, her cubby, and met the other kids in her class. Unbeknownst to me, Regal was taking it all in. I'm not sure when he got the idea, but one day he announced that he wanted to go to school. He was 7. As a team, we began to set goals for him that would help him to adapt to the school setting. Let me also say that school was not my goal for Regal. In my mind, he would be homeschooled for the duration of his education. But I had learned to pay attention to Regal and follow his lead. We built in more structure, more rules, and routines. We spent more time sitting at a desk and preparing him for classroom etiquette, like raising your hand and asking questions. We structured our home program more like school so that Regal could be more prepared.

This structure lent itself to more rules and action steps. It moved me more to the rigid side. We weren't playing with Regal like we used to, and I was not being intentional in *being*; I was doing. Then we decided to stop using the Son-Rise program, and began to use more of a school curriculum model. I began working with the school district to prepare Regal for entering the classroom. This was a shift for me. I allowed it to take me away from staying centered in the principles that had facilitated Regal's growth and development. It was the Son-Rise model—of celebrating, staying present, accepting and not judging, joining, giving him the control, and building a bridge—that had facilitated the results we had seen. I had to be intentional in making sure we focused on what was important. Although we were moving towards a more traditional school model, the principles used in our home program could be applied in any setting. It did not have to be either/or. It was possible to have both/and. I had to be very purposeful in remembering that.

I never thought that remembering to "be" would be an issue. But as humans, we have a propensity to forget anything after a while. Perhaps a better description would be that it fades into the background; it becomes a distant memory. Foundational routines and rituals are key. Little reminders and visual keys keep you focused on what is important. I had to choose to "be" on purpose. Committing to my morning ritual kept me grounded and reminded me that Regal's results were as a result of my "being." If I wanted to keep seeing results, I had to keep making it a priority, and choose to "be" on purpose. The way to accomplish this was to keep practicing it, regardless of the season in my life. Oftentimes, there is a desperation that motivates us to prioritize the intangibles; they must be continued when life isn't as complicated.

## Seeing the Invisible

As we move through our day-to-day monotony, you have to keep seeing what is not seen. Regal's goal to go to school came when he really did not appear that he could do it. He had come a long way, but he was still not ready for a regular classroom. Sure, he could go to school and be placed in a classroom with other special kids, but that was not the vision that he had for himself. He wanted to go to school like Nia. He wanted the experience like his sister. He was very specific about that.

We began to map out all of the things that he needed to learn in order to go to school. The list was exhaustive and, at a glance, could be overwhelming. But we did not look through the visible eye. Again, we made the choice to believe in spite of what we could see. We began to talk about school, and frame our conversations around his goals. For example, Regal had a love for words. He would go to bed at night reading the dictionary. He would then use the words in his conversations, but most of the time, the way he used them was understandable only to him. We would challenge him: "When you go to school, the kids will not understand what you mean. If you want to make friends, you will have to speak in a way that they understand you." When he was inflexible: "When you go to school, you will have to do things someone else's way; you can't have it your way."

I struggled at times. Was I trying to change him? Was I teaching him to become a different person in order to fit in? But ultimately, everyone needs to adapt to certain social norms in order to live in this world. So we continued to teach him about school behaviors. Even though he was not catching on quickly, we still chose to believe. We continued to encourage him to dream and envision himself in school, sitting in the classroom at his desk, and playing with other kids. We imagined together, Regal talking to his teacher and participating in assemblies. We talked about all of these things with him. We spoke in the affirmative, and we believed it would happen, because that was Regal's vision for himself.

## Watching and Waiting

We just kept at it—speaking and believing, teaching and adjusting, and watching what needed to be adjusted—waiting for the changes to take place so that Regal could participate in school. We started adding other children for Regal to practice with. I reached out to two friends and asked if their children could come and play with Regal on a weekly basis. Jack and Camryn had weekly play dates with Regal at the Social Enrichment Center. Beth, the founder, had been a part of our team since the inception of our home program. She and her team facilitated the playdates. Regal began to learn how to play with other kids. The kids did not give Regal control. Regal had to take turns. He had to listen to the kids and play games he didn't always want to play. He had to take turns, and he had to follow rules. We worked at this for two years.

The day arrived that Regal was ready to go to school. He started in the fourth grade for a half day in the afternoons. It was different than we imagined. Although we did everything we could on our end to get him ready, being in the actual classroom brought out other details we had not considered. There were so many new variables. Regal was bombarded with sensory stimulation just by virtue of being on school property; the large population of children, the architecture of the building, the classroom, the lights, the background noises that no one else seemed to notice, the bathrooms, the 20 other children, the teachers, the bells, the announcements... the list could go on and on. But he was there. He reached his goal. It took two years, but he did it.

Regal was not the only one adjusting. I had a new team to work with at the school—new people I had to listen to and learn from, and a new system to understand. These could have been overwhelming, and they would've been, 4 years ago. But time had taught me valuable lessons. Confidence was now a part of who I was. Even if I didn't understand, I knew I could figure it out. I had learned the value of people as resources. I knew that the new team was not against me; they were for Regal. However, I had to help them to see him the way I saw him. They did not know Regal. So I made it my job to make sure they understood who Regal was. As I helped them to understand Regal, I chose to believe that they were my allies for Regal. I was not combative with the team even if we didn't see eye to eye. I took time to understand their perspective. I patiently explained mine. I expected that we would come to a consensus for what was best for Regal. I sought to understand the framework. I learned the system. I continued to use my advocate to assist me in the process. I made sure that we worked together to help Regal reach his potential.

I know there are situations where school districts are not willing to work with the family. Keep fighting for your child. Find an advocate or a lawyer to get what you need for your child. For a list of advocates and special education lawyers, visit helloautismbook.com/ bonuses.

## Joy Unspeakable

Regal continued to adapt to his new learning environment. He worked with the social enrichment center in the morning and went to school in the afternoon. We continued to work on his goals for being a student. In January, he was ready to go for a full day. He was ecstatic; we all were. Being there all day would allow him to participate in the specials, like music and gym and attending assemblies. There were still gaps, and he struggled throughout the day with his classroom schedule. He was still writing in the air with his fingers throughout the day. He was impulsive and very much unaware of personal space. His conversations were extremely one-sided, and he was still very distracted by his environment, but the kids accepted him. If I visited the school, one of Regal's classmates would always tell me how cool he was, or how funny he was. As a matter of fact, whenever I met a parent of someone in Regal's class, they would thank me for allowing Regal to come to school. Regal was finding his way and making his mark, simply by being Regal.

# Takeaways

# Chapter Eleven

# Counting My Blessings

*"Sometimes you've got to let everything go—purge yourself. If you are unhappy with anything... whatever is bringing you down, get rid of it. Because you'll find that when you're free, your true creativity, your true self comes out."*
– Tina Turner

## Grateful for Autism

When I sat in the park with my husband, crying because Regal was kicked out of preschool, I had no idea what was in store for our family. When Regal was diagnosed with autism, I was devastated. I was scared. I was afraid of what the future held for my son. Would he have friends? Would he be able to have employment? Would he be accepted? Would I have to take care of him his whole life? Would he ever talk to us? Would he connect? Could I be a good mom? Could I advocate for him? Could I learn and grasp what I needed in order to be effective? Would we be able to afford it? If you are reading this book, I'm sure you resonate with these, and could probably add a dozen more.

Now, 15 years later, Regal is an honors student at his local HS. He has gotten several offers from prestigious colleges. He has a passion for the environment, with a vision to make an impact in the world and find solutions for sustainability. He consistently does his chores without any complaints. He washes dishes, makes his own lunch, cooks at least twice a week, washes everyone's clothes, vacuums, and washes the floors. He plays the piano and enjoys working out with his dad. He is insightful, kind, and caring.

It's not perfect. There are many things that he is still not able to do. There are still fears that I have for him, and questions and concerns. Regal is respected and admired, but he doesn't receive invitations to parties. Unlike his sister he does not have sleepovers, and he doesn't hang out with a crew. He still does things that I don't understand. He still has behaviors that people may feel uncomfortable with, like talking to himself very loudly. He's learned not to do that in public, only when he is home with family. He still writes in the air with his pointer finger when he talks to people. He still reads the dictionary and uses words in a way that doesn't always make sense to me. He doesn't understand abstract concepts and social cues. And he can get nervous and anxious over things that we wouldn't think twice about.

Regal takes things literally. Just recently, I got a call from his school because he hadn't checked in with the attendance office. I was concerned because to my knowledge he had gotten on the school bus that morning. I called him several times and he didn't answer the phone. I checked the tracker on his phone and saw that he was moving on school property. Before I could call the school to give them an update, they called to inform me that he had arrived at school. Why was Regal late? He had missed the bus and remembered that I told him the next time he misses the bus he was walking to school. I was joking at the time, but Regal took that literally. Instead of coming back inside to ask for a ride, he walked forty minutes to get to school.

Regal loves school, but he chooses to eat lunch alone, even though we have encouraged him to be open to his peers that have extended invitations over the years. He thinks friends will distract him from his studies (he may be right about that), but when he goes to college, he plans to make friends, because he wants a wife and seven kids. Yes, he is still doing things on his own terms, and he knows how to take care of himself.

He is the personification of his name: Regal. And I'm grateful for his life. He has changed me and my family. He has changed the lives of literally thousands of people that have been a part of the miracle, and for that, I am grateful.

Fifteen years later, I train women to stand in their power, and to turn their setbacks into comebacks. I've encouraged other moms of special needs kids to believe the best for their child. I am confident. I am a leader. I am strong. I love my life. I am grateful for autism; it taught me to love.

## Deep Relationships

As I sat so many times at the edge of my bed, weeping over Regal's diagnosis, I had no idea that I would inherit deep and meaningful relationships as a result of his diagnosis. I had no idea how rich my life would be. I did not know how many people would become a part of my community, and the deep relationships that would form. I have friends today that are still an integral part of my life that I developed because of Regal. They are people I know I would not have crossed paths with if not for autism. They have changed my life, shaped my views, and given me a broader perspective. I don't see them often, perhaps a few times a year at most. But the bond is deep, and it's real. We support each other, and we cry together. We share resources. I can call on them at any time, and we will have each other's back.

## Creating Spaces for Meaning

We worked long and hard with Regal to help him find his voice and communicate his needs and wants. Words have power. But Regal is also communicating when he is not speaking. Regal's life gives voice to persistence, diligence, and resilience. He personifies *miracle*. When he enters a room, he lets the world know that all things are possible.

We communicate powerfully when we create these spaces for our special kids. We empower them to be their authentic selves. It creates awareness, compassion, and understanding. These spaces facilitate meaningful conversations. Living in this way, gives others the permission to do so. It keeps you alive, vibrant, and focused on meaning and purpose.

These spaces challenge us to keep evolving, growing, and discovering who we really are. This opens us up to give more. This is our purpose for living, to receive love and give love, and to shine brightly in a world of darkness—to heal each other's wounds through the transformative power of love. Shallow is overrated. Commit to creating spaces for meaning.

## Making Memories

I've learned to approach every interaction as an opportunity to create a memory. I see every interaction with Regal as an opportunity to create a memory for him. A memory that impacts his way of thinking, his way of living, his confidence, and the way he shows up in the world, so that when people interact with him, he is unforgettable. And when they hear *autism*, they will think of Regal, and they will smile. They will be hopeful. When parents meet Regal, they will have hope. As a result of teachers working with Regal, they will change their approach when they have other special needs kids in their classrooms. Make memories with your child in such a way that it will be imprinted on their hearts. As such, they will leave an unforgettable impression on everyone they come into contact with.

## Takeaways

# Chapter Twelve

# Life Is Beautiful

*"You never know which experiences of life are going to be of value ...*
*You've got to leave yourself open to the hidden opportunities."*
– Robin Roberts

## Just Believe

I once wrote a song about the power of believing the best for your child. The chorus says:

*You can do, you can be, whatever path you choose*
*Who are they to say what's there inside of you*
*Choose to see and believe there is purpose; yes, indeed*
*Wait and see, it will be so beautiful*
*Just believe*

You have the power to create what you want for your child. You have the power to create what you want for your family. You have the power to create what you want for your life. You are not limited by your environment, your community, or a diagnosis. You were given an amazing gift; all human beings have it. It is called resourcefulness—the ability to find quick and clever ways to overcome difficulties. Some are naturally better at this than others, but we all have it. We just have to practice using it. Create what you want.

Build a better environment for your child so they can thrive. Cultivate a supportive community so you can thrive. Study, learn, and ask questions so that you will know what is available. Invest in yourself, and expand your capacity to love. Develop your faith muscle. You become what you believe. If you think your life is over, then it is over. If you think this is the worst thing that has ever happened to you, then that is what it will be. Yes, there is pain. You will be stretched beyond measure. But you are strong—you really are—and your child is going to show you just how strong you are. Don't give up. Please don't give up. Keep committing. Keep choosing to fight, and keep choosing to believe.

## Keep Committing

Your child is an amazing human being. They were given to you to help you for a purpose. You won't see or know the purpose immediately. It has many aspects, and many turns and twists that you can't plan for—many that you will never feel prepared for. But it is good, because it directs our hearts to the invisible part of who we are. At the center of it all is love. This journey with your special child expands your capacity to love. Everything is better when it has been touched by love. Commit to the process, with the knowledge that you are being transformed into a better person every time you interact with and for your child.

Put the principles into practice, one at a time. Try it out. If something doesn't work, then move on to the next thing. Keep growing, keep adding to this template, and let it work for you. There is always a solution. It's your choice. You can love, like (enjoy), and learn from your child. Love wins. Always.

## Life is Beautiful

A colleague recently shared the experience of author, John Elder Robison. Robison, an adult with ASD, participated in a transcranial magnetic stimulation (TMS) clinical trial. He writes in his book, *Switched On: A Memoir of Brain Change and Emotional Awakening*, how his life changed when his emotions switched on. Robison became aware of the world around him and began to live in a very different way. For the first time in his life, he was able to experience empathy, read nonverbal cues, and see the pain in people's eyes. The ever autism warrior for my son, I started doing research and located a treatment center in our area that was willing to administer TMS for autism. Currently, TMS is only approved for depression and anxiety.

I discussed the treatment with my husband, Henry, and he was concerned about how it could change Regal. Regal is happy. Although he has had challenges, he is happy. Pretty much the only time Regal isn't happy is if he is physically ill. But for the most part, he is always singing, laughing to himself, and enjoying his life. When we asked him if he would consider the therapy, he said no. I asked why. His answer was, "I like myself. I like my life. I don't want to change it."

Was I disappointed? Yes. But it's not my life. Regal is happy. His world is beautiful. He touches everyone around him and makes them better. Whenever Regal has wanted to change something in his life, he does it. I respect that. We have given him the tools to go after what he wants. His life is beautiful.

What I want most for my children is for them to know their purpose and live their best life, to the fullest on their terms. I want them to be kind. I want them to be thoughtful. I want them to love God, love others, and love themselves. Regal is well on his way to checking all the boxes. I choose to accept who he is and to let go of my attachment to a particular outcome or result. I live with gratitude over who he has become, and celebrate who he is.

As long as you are breathing, there is an opportunity for you and your child to grow. Both of you are not done growing until you take your last breath. Look for the good. Believe the best. Commit to learning from your child. You will grow in strength, love and enjoyment while creating beautiful memories along the way.

## Takeaways

If you would like to go deeper into the principles presented in this book, my #HelloLife Trainings for women would be a great resource for you. Please visit www.theresanoye.com for more information.

## Acknowledgements

I would like to first thank my husband, **Henry J. Noye**. KMB, you bring out the woman in me, and I am grateful for our partnership. Thank you for your love, encouragement, and support. We've built a whole life together, and we have only just begun.

To my son, **Regal Aaron Noye**, it is an honor to be your mom. Loving you is easy cause you're beautiful. Thank you for teaching me how to be a present, powerful, and patient woman.

To my daughter, **Nia Alexandra Noye**, I love you. I love you more. I love you most. I love you longer. I love you forever. You make me a better woman. Thank you for sharing your life with me.

To my mother, **Rev. Webster Blades-Israel**, whenever I am with you, I learn something new. You are amazing, Mommy. Thank you for loving me so well.

To my sister, **Shanita Blades**, you are my best sister. Thank you for reminding me what it means to be a sister.

To my brother, **Michael Blades**, you are always in my heart.

**Cheryl Ott**, my best good friend. I can't imagine my life without you in it. You have taught me what it means to be a friend. I love you to life. Have I told you lately how much I appreciate you?

**Pastor Gabriel Bouch** and my **Freedom Church family:** I just love FCP. Where else can you have weekly conversations with people from all over the world? Thanks for loving me and my family.

**Pastors Clarence and Ja'Ola Walker,** and **Fresh Anointing Christian Center**: You walked with us through some of our most difficult moments. Thank you for your love, prayers, and support.

**Melissa Bilash**, thank you for teaching, supporting, and advocating for us.

**Radnor Township School District**: I am grateful for your investment in our son. Regal has been welcomed and supported with excellence from the time he entered school in the 4th grade. He loves school, and I have always felt like I was on a team. Thank you.

**Maureen Leo**, you have been an excellent resource and champion for Regal. Thank you for your partnership.

**Our Home Program Community:** There are so many people that volunteered in our home program, consistently, for six years. Hundreds of people gave their time and resources over the years, and I am grateful for your presence in our lives.

**Beth Roberts**, thank you for loving Regal like he was your own.

**Char Nolan**, you befriended me as I wandered around Whole Foods in an overwhelmed daze. You embraced our family and became my number one cheerleader. Thank you for always believing in me.

**Dr. Joe Schneider,** your knowledge, expertise, and commitment to our family were invaluable. Thank you.

**Bob Anderson and Beth Johnson**, AKA Aunt Beth and Big Bad Bob, your kindness and love for our family will never be forgotten. Thank you.

**Jeff & Jenifer Westphal**, your generosity and support will always be remembered. You are beautiful human beings.

**Candyce Wilson**, your encouragement to "keep getting up every morning" moved me forward. Thanks for keeping your door open, my glass full, and my heart lifted.

Brown Skin Girls—**Adelaide, Brittanie, Jess, Pannan, Tiff, and Toya**—our sister circle is a healing balm. "Read!" "Import!"

**Nicky Mendez**, thanks for always being there and sharing your knowledge and expertise. You are a beast. I love you, Mama!

**Hampton University**: My life changed the day I arrived at my Home by the Sea. I am thankful for the friendships that span well over 30 years, and for the new relationships that are easily formed, simply because we are Hamptonians. Our lives are doing the singing, and it is a beautiful symphony. A special shout out to my **Genesis II** classmates.

**Gamma Iota Sorors of Delta Sigma Theta Sorority, Inc:** *Let me tell you 'bout the G-A-M-M-A...* You are so beautiful to me. There are no words. Thank you.

**Untouchables Spr'88**: Linesisters, thank you for always having my back.

**Jenny McCarthy** and **Holly Robinson Peete,** who publicly shared their journey about their children. Your transparency gave me hope and confidence to believe for my son.

Finally, I want to thank the **Eastern University** community. Our family lived on campus for nearly 25 years. During that time, we have been loved, embraced, and cared for by faculty, staff, and students alike. There are far too many angels from this community to name, as they would span the length of this entire book. Some are no longer with us; others have transitioned to other jobs; there are students that have graduated; and there are people in the community that continue to be an integral part of our lives. I thank God every time I think of each of you. A special mention to **Bettie Ann Brigham,** whose support allowed me to continue to work and run our home program. I also want to give a shout out to the residents of **Kea-Guffin**—one love, one faith, one hall—KG forever.

## About Theresa

Theresa is the founder of #HelloLife Coaching. She helps ambitious women live life with passion and joy by creating a personalized system that transforms negative thoughts into achievable goals. Theresa is committed to empowering women to step out of the shadows and make the impact they were destined for.

Theresa is a proud native of Brooklyn, NY, currently living in Wayne, PA. She has been married to Henry J. Noye, Esq. for over 20 years. They have two teenagers, Regal and Nia, and a rabbit, Buddy the Elf. She loves shoes, experiencing new cultures and meaningful conversations.

If you would like to have Theresa facilitate a training, speak at your next Women's Event, or to participate in one of her #HelloLife Coaching Programs, visit www.theresanoye.com.

CPSIA information can be obtained
at www.ICGtesting.com
Printed in the USA
BVHW042011260720
584445BV00007B/21

9 798637 864270